MY LIFE
AND
30 SECONDS WITH A PARAMEDIC

Victor M. Torrens

My Life and 30 Seconds with a Paramedic
Copyright © Victor M. Torrens, 2020
First published October 2020

ISBN: 978-0-6487555-5-5 E-Book
ISBN: 978-0-6487555-4-8 Paperback

All rights reserved. Without limiting the rights under copyright reserved above, no part of this publication may be reproduced, stored in or introduced into a database and retrieval system or transmitted in any form or by any means (electronic, mechanical, photocopying, recording or otherwise) without the prior written permission of the owner of the copyright.

Original illustrations/ Photographs by Victor M. Torrens.

Published with the assistance of Angel Key Publications.
angelkey.com.au

A catalogue record for this book is available from the National Library of Australia

INTRODUCTION

This is a story of a young boy from a poor family, who eventually had a very interesting career. A career that lasted a lifetime. The stories told are short. I trust that you find them as interesting to read, as I found them interesting to be involved in. My whole paramedic career was controlled by my dedication to my patients, and my faith in a God who allows us to help other people, in their adversity. I have on a lot of occasions shed tears with my patients and their families and also privately. I have also had many good laughs with some patients, "laughter is the best medicine". I would like to sincerely thank my dear wife, Heather and our three children, Rose, Alan and Nigel. For their patience and understanding during my career, there were many times I was not available for birthdays and other special events in their lives. I hope the love I have shown for them has helped in this regard. I also thank God through whom I have received the power, patience and dedication to work through the many types of adversity I had in my career. The seeds of my life have been sown.

Enjoy my memories as much as I have.

About the Author

One Birth and a Family

This is a collection of memories and stories from the life of Victor M. Torrens.

The story begins with my birth at Nambour, Queensland, on the 4th November, 1944. I was apparently born as the clock was striking midnight between the 4th and 5th of November. Mum's birthday was on the 4th of November, and she was asked what day she would like my birthday to be. I am glad that she chose the 4th as it has always been a reminder of the love that Mum has shown me and all my siblings throughout her life.

I was the middle child in a family of 10 children. Mum had a miscarriage at about 1952 which would have been a girl. Phillip, my youngest brother, was born after this.

These are my siblings in order of their birth.
- Keith   11-11-1934
- John   07-07-1940
- Ian   22-01-1942
- Cecil   21-08-1943
- Victor   04-11-1944
- Lillian   17-12-1945
- Jeffrey   24-06-1947
- Cynthia   14-10-1948
- Sylvia   02-04-1950
- Phillip   09-04-1955

The earliest memories I have of my childhood are sketchy although a few things do stand out.

Walking to pictures

Some time when I think I was about 13 months old, Mum, Dad and some of us were going to the pictures at Maroochydore. It was a great event. I remember being pushed in the pram when Cecil, who was very chubby at the time, complained that he did not want to walk, so I was taken out of the pram, and I had to walk. Cecil got a ride in the pram but he was too big to carry that far.

Game time

I can remember playing *Monopoly* with some family members including Grandma Torrens in their house on the esplanade at Maroochydore. I think it would have been in 1948. The house was not directly on the esplanade but setback, sort of behind and between two other houses which were directly on the esplanade. It was a high house with fibro walls and slats underneath. Grandma Torrens died at about 1949 from bowel cancer for which she had several operations before her death, I remember that she was nicknamed "wirebelly" because of it.

Cubby house & carpet snake

In my first year at school I remember going to an old rubbish dump on the way to Alexandra Headlands looking for materials so that I could make a cubby house. We did find a sheet of old lino, but while lifting it up we spotted a large carpet snake. We instantly forgot about the lino, the cubby house, and everything else as we rushed home. That was a truly exciting experience.

Cutting my foot after school

I had a good time when I was in school even though I was never a great student. I loved to daydream, but never about anything specific. I find that I am still like this. Sometimes

I can just shut everything off and have a completely blank mind with nothing in my head at all. I have several memories from my school days at Maroochydore. One time as we were going home from school, we passed through a nearby billboard advertising Holden cars for sale. We had a lot of fun pelting rocks at the sign to try and bend it. I remember getting too close to pelt a rock that I ended up badly cutting my foot on broken glass. My brother Ian piggybacked me home and Aunty Grace bandaged my foot. I ended up at the doctor who was in a little shop on the esplanade but he was unable to stitch the wound, which was shaped like a tablespoon under my big toe. My leg had to be put in plaster and it was like that for several weeks. I did enjoy it though as I could get away with a lot of things by "bunging it on a bit." I was also pushed around in the pram from time to time. Until today I still get some problems with the scarring on my foot.

Deaf teacher

One of our teachers at Maroochydore, Mr. Slater, was quite deaf and this gave us some fun at his expense. We would throw our nib pens at the ceiling and see if it would stick into the plaster. Sometimes it did and sometimes it didn't. Poor old Mr. Slater would try and catch us but he never did. We would always have an excuse for the noise, for example someone would cough or sneeze to cover up the sound of the pen hitting the ceiling. He was a good teacher, and I learned many things from him related to sticking to a task. I had him for years 1 and 2.

At the office

Mr. O'Brien who was the headmaster at Maroochydore was also a good teacher but he was a cranky old coot. One time, we were pelting rocks at the big sign down the road when he came storming after us, ready to hit us all with his cane. Someone yelled out "Here comes old O'Brien!" so he was not able to catch us then. Next morning however, he lined us all up and he gave us the cane for calling him "old O'Brien." There were about 10 or 12 of us. He was a master with the cane and we always left with our hands ringing after getting punished, even if we used the old *Brylcreem* on the fingers trick. While on our trip around Australia in 2007, we spent a week at Carnarvon where I was able to talk to a chap who grew oranges. It turned out that he went to school at Maroochydore and his grandfather was Mr. O'Brien. I had good friends at Maroochydore. One of them was Cyril Grieg, who died in an accident near Caloundra turnoff when he was 17 for driving too fast in his first car which I think was a DeSoto Dodge V8.

A scary time

Another lad we got along well with was Cyril Smith, he was part Aboriginal, and he was easily spooked. One time, I was walking home from school with Cyril Grieg and Cyril Smith. Grieg and I decided that we will frighten Smith by telling him some stories about spooks and things. We really got him going, and he was real upset and balling his eyes out when we reached his house. He raced in and told his mother what we were doing, and she got cranky, and I mean *cranky*. She went after us with a dirty great machete threatening to chop us up. Talk about how the tables have turned. It was now time for me and Cyril Grieg to get out of there. Cyril Grieg made it safe to his house, and I thought I did too. Mrs. Smith was breathing down my neck as I reached my house, but the door was locked, and no one was home! So I headed out to the dunny and locked myself inside, while Mrs Smith ranted and raved around outside while banging on the door and threatening me with all sorts of terrible things. I guess this time I was the one who was scared witless and was balling his eyes out. She eventually left after quite some time, and

I was still in the dunny when mum got home, but I did not tell her what happened. We then copped it the next day at school. More cuts. Cyril Smith and I were best mates after that episode.

Dad cutting timber at Maroochydore

Dad was a timber cutter/tree feller who enjoyed his work, and he was good at it. I remember spending time with him in his camp somewhere near the southern end of Fisherman's road as it is now, near Maroochydore. There was a tent for sleeping in and a lean-to type structure made from timber and bark where the cooking fire was made. There was always plenty of tea, bread, and syrup or dripping to be eaten, and we always had porridge for breakfast. Until now I still love porridge made from rolled oats. We slept on an old camp stretcher with a fibre mattress, which was not that comfortable, but I still slept well.

Dad was able to look at a tree standing in the bush, walk around it, and then estimate, always accurately, the amount of timber in super feet that would be milled from the log. I have also seen Dad check out a stand of scrub that he was to clear, by walking around in it and sizing up the trees, looking at which way they would fall, then cutting belly marks in the trees, one by one, with specific angles made to the cuts. Eventually, he would fall one of the trees, and the effect was similar to dominoes, and by just cutting this one tree down at the right angle he could clear several acres of scrub, ready for burning.

Dad was a master at his chosen career, he loved axes and axemanship, and he would spend hours honing his axes. Sometimes us kids would chop chips and wood with his axes and promptly ruin all his good work. He would give us a touch up with a waddy or razor strop, then redo the axe. He competed in many chopping competitions against the likes of Vic Summers and the Grieg brothers. Dad had his share of wins at these competitions. I entered a few competitions but never did well.

Rampaging goanna.

One time Dad, I and Uncle Walter were cutting timber near Fisherman's road at Maroochydore. They were camped in a tent, where all their bedding, tucker, and clothes were. There was a large goanna there which made a habit of coming into the tent when everyone was away and eating the tucker. Uncle Walter and Dad spoke about trapping it and they decided that Uncle Walter would set the trap, which was to be a noose set so that the goanna would put his neck through and then it would tighten around his neck. The goanna was to be taken away from the campsite and set loose if it was caught. Uncle Walter set the trap well and caught the goanna. There was one small problem though, he had anchored the rope to the tent peg. The poor goanna got caught and set about trying to escape but only succeeded in demolishing the tent and everything else in sight. What a mess!

Timber!

There was a time at Tanawha when Dad was clearing some country to plant bananas and I brought his smoko over just as he was ready to fall a big Blackbutt tree. I cooeed as was our practice to let him know we were there. He called me closer down the hill and assured me that all was well and the tree would be falling away from my direction. When the tree started to fall it came towards me and of course I took off, spilling the smoko all over the country. The tree was about 100 yards from where I was standing and would never have reached me in a fit, but being a little fellow then I had no grasp of distance. Dad thought of it as a great joke. I had to go and get some more smoko.

Maroochydore

Grandpa and Grandma Torrens lived on the Esplanade at Maroochydore, mid-way between Cotton Tree and Cornmeal Creek. In the backyard were several large gum trees which gave us some shade from the heat. Sometime around 1951 or 1952, we were playing under the trees when four Canberra Bombers came roaring overhead, they were so low that they trimmed some of the branches off the tops of these trees and us kids were scared so bad that we all dived under the neighbour's house which was very low to the ground. I know it would not offer any protection but a kid does not know this and we reckoned it was a safe place.

Raiding the orange patch

Near the mouth of Cornmeal Creek just around the Maroochy Sands shopping centre there lived a Chinaman who was a market gardener. He grew chooks, oranges, mandarins and a bunch of other stuff. This garden was surrounded by a large, thick hedge of Lantana, I suppose to protect the crops. Several of us town kids had made tracks through this Lantana to the garden and we would delight in swiping fruits to eat. The old Chinaman would try and catch us and threatened us with instant death if he caught us, but he never did. He would chase us into the Lantana and we would lose him as we swam across the creek.

Sad time

At one time a plump friend of ours was playing on the top storey of their house when he fell off the veranda and landed on a broomstick which went right through him. It was awful. He died.

Drunk

We once found a drunk man sleeping on the edge of Cornmeal Creek and we decided to wake him up with a bucket of water. Boy was it funny when he tried to chase us, he kept falling over and threatening to take us home to our parents for a flogging.

At war

One of our best pastimes at Maroochydore was playing war with bobby dazzlers. Two teams would face each other on the creek banks and pelt clay balls at each other, and if you got hit you were out of the game. It was great fun playing that game. A bobby-dazzler is a twitchy stick about three feet long where a ball of clay is placed on the end and thrown at your opponent. They can travel a fair distance and sting if they hit.

Shopping for Mum

I remember one time when Mum sent me to the shop to buy a loaf of bread and gave me just the right amount of money for it. On the way to the store I pinched a little red chilli pepper from someone's garden, boy-o-boy was it hot. I raced to the shop and bought some ice cream to try and stop the burning. I guess it helped, but then I had no money for bread and got a licking for my trouble. On another occasion I think Ian and Cecil were sent to get a loaf of bread and a bar of soap, then on the way home, they ate the centre out of the bread and stuffed the bar of soap inside. This did not work for them, and they got a licking for their efforts.

Learning a trade

One time, Ian and John were enjoying themselves painting the inside of the dunny with the contents of the can. It was not a very nice pastime, but it resulted in them packing their bags and leaving home. I did not know where they were going. They were about 6 or 7 years old, I think.

Mangoes and fishing

We loved to go over to Goat Island near Maroochydore at Christmas time and raiding the mango trees there. There were a lot of them there and a few hundred or maybe even thousands of flying foxes. One time we were fishing with Dad in a small boat, I don't exactly remember who was there, but some of us kids were with him, and we got onto a patch of whiting, and we were literally scooping them from the water into the boat by hand. We must have caught dozens of them before we went home. There was also a time when I caught a big mullet by hand in the seaweed near the fish bait shop at the esplanade. Uncle Mick said that the thing must have been sick, so we filled the bathtub up with water and let it swim around. I reckon it was asleep when I caught it. We had a good feed off of it anyhow.

Hungry at Tanawha

There was rarely a lot to eat in the Torrens household, but we always got by. Mum could cook anything that was available. I remember one time we were down to custard powder and pumpkin, so we had pumpkin flavoured custard and pumpkin leaf stems, like beans, for tea. We always managed to have something to eat even if it was only toast and dripping, which is a good meal when you are hungry. Dad once worked for a baker at Caloundra, he was cutting cord wood which was a lot of hard work. He would often come home with a sack bag of old bread, and we would have bread and milk. It was a tasty meal with the bread we had back in the day but it's not as good with the refined bread of today.

Eating our fruit

During our time at Tanawha we grew bananas and sometimes small crops and watermelons. Us kids would love to have Cavendish banana eating competitions, and I always enjoyed this as I love bananas. We would sit in a circle with a heap of bananas and peel about 30 each and then on the count of 5 we would start eating. The winner would receive a banana as a prize. When it was watermelon season we would help pick them and load them onto the truck so that they could be sold at the market. I am talking about watermelons which were up to three feet long and probably weighed 50-80 pounds. It was a common occurrence that one would get dropped as we were carrying them and of course this would split it and we would then have to eat it. This was always a real treat as they were always sweet sugary melons.

Monsters

Near where we grew the melons at about 300 yards from the house, there was an old plywood hut used by farm visitors and occasionally us kids would camp there overnight. One night we were asleep and Dad came down with a .303 gun and let off a couple of rounds in the air, which frightened us kids. Dad told us that there was a monster there which had a wheel on its tail to keep it off the ground. Until today I still don't know what it was but I assume that it was the old plough which we used to pull with the horses. At any rate we sure believed it to be a monster and that dad had fought it and won. He was a hero for sure.

Glory box

The house we lived in had a timber weather board exterior and beautiful tongue and groove white and red cedar floors and lining. Our home had no ceiling and I kept my treasure in a wooden box nailed to the top of the partitions. This box contained chewing gum, pencils, my favourite marbles and some other "valuables." Unfortunately, my siblings used to raid this box and knock everything off if I wasn't able to catch them.

Dogs

We nearly always had a dog and one dog which stood out was Laddie. I didn't know what breed he was but he was a faithful white dog who was about two feet high and boy could he run. We used to race him using our pushbikes and he would always win. I remember one time he was chasing me and I suddenly stopped then he jumped clean right over me. He was a legend from then on. There was also a time when he was attacked by some dingos, which were always plentiful. I think dad got about 1 Pound ($2.00) for their scalps at Landsborough. Laddie was attacked by the pack and I guess he gave them a run for their money but he was badly wounded and he crawled under the laundry floor. We weren't able to find him for three days and we had to rip the floor up to treat him. Another time, he came home and was very badly burned because someone threw hot water at him and it took him a long time to recover from that. I also remember when he came with us to Maroochydore during the holidays. When we were about to go home he went missing and it took about seven weeks before he eventually got back to Tanawha which was about a 12 to 14-mile walk for him. He was starved and worn out when he got home. He eventually just wandered off and we assumed that he died although the dingos may have got him again.

Trapping dingos

Dad was a very good dingo trapper and tracker. He would find out where their lair was and set up a blind and at about either daylight or dusk he would set himself up and call the dingos by howling. The dingos would literally walk right up to Dad and he would just shoot them then scalp them and we would eat again with the proceeds of the sale. We were often hungry but we never starved. Mum had the ability to make a meal out of very little and she did this often.

Boxing/sport

I spent about three years boxing when I was 12-15 years old. I remember getting beaten in the Golden Gloves semis, although I was never knocked out and I did not get marked in any way. One fight I had at Caboolture was fairly difficult for me because earlier in the day my left big toe got caught in the chain sprocket of a fixed wheel bike and ripped it open. I had to fight barefoot that night. I lost. I probably was not good enough that time. On this same day my cousin Hedley and I made some milk ice blocks to celebrate the fight. I put a lot of green colouring in the mixture and when they were frozen Hedley was convinced that I had put arsenic in the milk. He refused to have them and even took some of them to the ambulance so that it could be analysed to make sure that they were edible. We ended up throwing them out though. We stayed up all throughout that night with a fire going on a sheet of corrugated iron on the lawn of Uncle Bill Adams', Hedley's dad's, house. If you knew Uncle Bill and his love for gardening, you knew that the lawn was beautiful. We figured that if we put the tin under the fire it would not burn the grass, but boy were we wrong. Irene and her twin sister Jan were in the house and warned us several times that we would be in strife. We reckoned we'd be alright but we were proven wrong. I had a great time when I was boxing. I enjoyed it and made some very good friends such as my trainer Sam Tomlinson, and his sons Gary and Noel or "Hookey." Gary was a good boxer. I also enjoyed a lot of other sports, such as running, wrestling and tennis. I won several trophies playing on grass and clay in the Palmwoods junior tennis competition. These were the days of Rod Laver's beginnings as a champion.

Boy scouts

I joined the scouts at Buderim and had a great time with them throughout several years. The leader was Fred Leek and his wife Connie. I came across them many years later in a fruit orchard when I was appointed to Stanthorpe in 1983. We got fruit from them often. Fred died of cancer while I was in Stanthorpe. I had the opportunity to transport him on several occasions just before his death. I went to his funeral at Wallangarra. During one scout camp we were given the task of counting headstones in the Buderim cemetery, a scary task for an 11 year old. Still, away we went and while we were there we met our first "ghost." I don't know who it was but it was a fair dinkum ghost who scared our pants off. I reckon I ran a four-minute mile twice to get back to camp about 8 miles away. And this was about the time John Landy was doing great things with miles and times. He would have been proud of me. On our scout camps someone would be tasked with cooking the meal for the troop, which had about 12 to 15 of us. When it was my turn I was given a box of veges, a two-pound packet of SR flour, a big pot, and I was told to cook a stew for tea. Nothing to it, I thought. So in went all the veges, rice and other ingredients. When it was well-cooked and slowly simmering over the fire, it was time to put the flour in to thicken it a bit. I had used all the veges and other ingredients so I assumed I would use all the flour as well, so I mixed it up and put the lot into the pot. It looked good, the veges were all soft and well-cooked. The only problem was that it was so thick it could not be removed from the pot. I was not asked to cook again for that camp and we had baked beans and toast for tea that night.

Shark

There was a time when I was training for boxing, and I used to swim several miles daily in the Maroochy River. The mouth of the river was different then, it was located more towards the Cotton Tree area. There was a big diving platform in the middle of the river, and we had many hours of fun here. I was swimming with a mate once when we spotted a shark, or maybe it was a dolphin, underneath us. Nevertheless, we did not wait around to see. I was still swimming about thirty feet up the beach out of the water. I enjoyed swimming and bodysurfing at Maroochydore, it was great fun.

My first job after school

Merv Ross was a good friend of mine who was also my boss for two years. He was a timber getter. We cut timber around Nambour, Tanawha, and Montville. One time we were cutting in the mountains and had to roll the logs over a cliff about 150 to 200 feet high. The idea was to have them land without smashing, and we had a success rate of about 90%. We then had to sing the logs again to a loading ramp. It was hard work, but I enjoyed it, and I guess it helped me grow up to be a strong young man with some tenacity. I remember once falling a tree which fell over an old log then it had to have its head cut off. I was tasked to do this and I promptly literally went "out on a limb" with axe in hand and commenced to cut the head off. With the tree bent slightly over the old log I was in for a shock as it turned out, because when I cut through the head the rest of the tree threw me upwards as the pressure was taken off and I went flying with no parachute. I was probably about 12 to 15 feet up in the air, my body going up one way, the axe going another. I fortunately had no injuries.

Restumping.

One time I was driving the old Canadian Blitz used for snigging logs out of the bush. While going past the house, the accelerator stuck, as it often would, and I lost control of the blitz for a short time and I managed to knock out the corner stump of the house. This stump was the one under Mum and Dad's bedroom. The truck was luckily not damaged but my ego unfortunately was.

Killing chooks

One time at Tanawha we were at the Tomlinsons' house. It was only us kids because the parents were away. They had several chooks running around and we delighted in throwing green guavas at them. We were pretty straight with our aim. I threw a guava and hit one of the chooks fair on the head. One dead chook was very quickly buried and the foxes were blamed the next day for it.

Gary's toe

Gary's dad used to have draft horses which were used for snigging logs out of the swampy areas. Gary would sometimes work them and one time he was stood on by one of the horses and his toes were severely damaged. He was taken to hospital without a murmur even though he was in terrible pain. He had not shed a tear until the nurses started to take his clothes off. He was a lad of about 12 then and the indignity of being undressed by females was more painful than the horse injury. He lost a toe in this accident.

Tanawha, farm, snakes, and rocks

In 1951 or 1952, we moved from Maroochydore to a banana farm in Tanawha. Dad shared with Billy Hughes who owned the place which measured about 1 square mile or 640 acres. There was quite a variety of country in this farm, and we kids enjoyed our time there. The farm had a creek flowing through it and we loved it when the rains came and filled the creek so we could swim for miles down the current. There was steep country at the back with many large rocks, and on several occasions, we kids would roll large rocks down the hills. We had great fun as they smashed into trees and other bigger rocks. Down the front there was a good patch of scrub with palm trees, lawyer cane, and much "monkey vine." This was good country for playing in although there were snakes aplenty; big carpet snakes, whip snakes, brown, tiger and black snakes and a few death adders. Dad always told us to never hit a snake with a stick, particularly death adders as they could curl around the stick and when you lifted it for a second whack the snake could slide down the stick and "gotcha." I received a good towelling up from Dad for doing this one time when I was about 11. A lesson well learnt because I have never hit a snake with a stick since then. From then on I used wire, and it is very effective. Dad taught me much about bushcraft that I have remembered and used often throughout my life. I thank him for that.

Billy Hughes, farm produce, explosions and other things

Billy Hughes was a bit of a character in his own right. He was an accountant or tax agent, though he was already retired, and he was not up to doing the work of a farm. When Dad first went to this farm, he lived in an old army donga made of plywood. There were two of them with a galley in between, and occasionally some of us kids were allowed to stay on holidays which was great fun. Dad grew water melons, Indian fruit, and other small crops so we nearly always had something to eat. Some of the watermelons were large enough that two people had to carry them. Indian fruit are no longer available, but they were delicious fruit grown on a rockmelon-like vine. The fruit was about 8 to 12 inches and long yellow in colour. It would split open when ripe, and you could smell them all over the house.

Life at Tanawha farm

The Tanawha house was up on a hill facing east and was overlooking Billy Hughes' house which was built almost inside the palm tree swamp. Water was always a problem, and we always had to carry buckets of water up from the creek for our washing and bathing. We got drinkable water from a hole we had dug out by hand. One time while we were there, Billy Hughes dug a well with our assistance. The well was dug by hand to about 30 feet deep through mainly clay and some sandstone which required blasting, which dad was able to do because he was a powder monkey. The well however almost always dry. We would often blow up stumps for a patch of bananas. This was always an exciting time as we would watch dad put the fuse in then he would make us hide behind a log or a big stump a long way from the gelignite. Dad would then light the fuse and run like mad to get to us before the thing blew up. We had to count how many blasts there were so that we knew when they had all gone off. I remember one time when one did not go off, and Dad did not go near the spot until the next day.

There was always plenty of work to do on the farm, like chipping, picking and packing bananas, and cutting firewood for our own use and also to sell. There were times when we would cut one block of wood using a crosscut saw before going to school and then cut more when we got home. Some of these logs were 4-5 feet through, and Dad would sell the wood in Nambour, Maroochydore, and Caloundra to keep us fed and clothed. Dad always worked hard to support us, but he never really had a long-term permanent job, like most timber cutters in those days. Dad would work at anything to earn a quid. He built bridges around Nambour and Wandoan. He also cut timber for the old Hornibrook Bridge. Most of these timbers were dressed by hand with the broad-axe, which dad was good at. Dad was a good axeman who taught me how to use the broad-axe. One time we spent 10 hours cutting a huge tree down. Dad and John did most of the work though I remember helping with the particular job. The tree was an old flooded gum, which was cut and used to build a bridge across the creek on our property's road. From what I remember, the tree was around 33 feet in girth when we cut it.

Need a hand

An interesting item of bush ingenuity was the dumb sawyer. This was achieved by placing a pole in the ground on the opposite side of the log to the one worker who would use the crosscut saw. A large rubber band made from an old tire tube would be connected to the handle of the crosscut and then hooked to the pole at the right height and position. One worker would then commence to use the crosscut saw and the rubber band would pull the saw back after the stroke was finished. This worked very effectively and allowed one person to cut through a log. A crosscut saw should only be used to cut when it is pulled, never when it is pushed, therefore this system was able to work.

Migrants

Billy Hughes at one time was involved in the migration of a family from somewhere in Europe. I think they were from Hungary. There was a mother and two girls. I think the idea was that Billy would marry the mother and support the family. It did not work though as they only remained at the farm for a couple of weeks and then disappeared. I remember that one of the girls was very athletic and could do all sort of acrobatic tricks. We used to watch her, but we weren't able to talk to her because no one among them could speak English. I think that Billy had misled them to some degree as I am sure that they expected to live in a city or at least a big town, not out in the bush with a lot of other bush kids.

Shooting motor cars

Billy had an old Morris car with a canvas hood that he used for his trips to town. We knew how to make arrows that could be propelled for several hundred metres if the correct shaft and throwing action was used. One time I threw an arrow from our house and it fairly flew straight as a die through the top of Billy's car and into the seat. He was not amused. He was also not amused when several of us painted his bathroom with red clay while we were using his house when he was away one day. He had us scrub the whole house from top to bottom. Best clean it ever had I reckon.

Sport & the Olympic torch

During our time at Tanawha the Olympics were held at Melbourne in 1956. A call was made for runners of the Olympic torch, which was carried all the way down the east coast of Queensland. Most of the kids from Buderim School put up their hand and only some of them were chosen. During this event the Olympic torch was carried all the way by runners who ran for a mile each. The torch was made of brass and the flame was kept going by using asbestos soaked in kerosene and diesel. There was a backup flame in the back of the support truck, and there were about four or five vehicles in the convoy when it came through Tanawha in late June 1956. I ran with the torch after receiving it from Jimmy Briers who lived just up the road from us. We had to wear white shirts and shorts and sandshoes. One of the criteria for carrying the torch was that you had to be able to cover the mile in under 7 minutes. I was at that time running the mile in about 5.50 minutes as I was in training for boxing and also swimming. I was chosen for the Queensland titles for swimming in backstroke and freestyle. I was not good enough to win but I did my best. I also lost most of my clothes at the swim meet at the valley pool, as did most of the other kids from our area. Someone knocked them off and we had to borrow from the people we were billeted with. I enjoyed my time throughout these years of my involvement in the sports of boxing, swimming, running and tennis. I think these years of training and playing have allowed me to be fairly competitive and remain coordinated throughout my life.

Goanna meal

One time Ian, Cecil and I went dingo hunting in the meridian plains at Sippy Creek. We took longer than expected and as a result we got very hungry. We came across an old dingo hide which was being eaten by a goanna then we treed the goanna and shot it. We then started a fire and cooked the goanna over the fire and ate its tail and back legs, it was very much like dry chicken. Thanks to the goanna we did not starve on our way home.

Christmas on the farm

Christmas on the farm was always a great time even though we would never get much presents. We always had a good Christmas dinner and there were always small presents, as far as Mum and Dad could afford. Marbles were always in the stocking and everyone would always have a great time playing poison, with plenty rivalries being formed during these times. Even the girls would leave their little dolls and line up to watch us. We would play marbles until Christmas dinner was served and what a feast it would be, hot meat, plenty of vegies, and a great massive plum pudding with custard. After dinner, the marbles would commence again until at some point dad would appear eating a slice of watermelon, which would put an immediate stop to the marbles for the afternoon as we would invariably end up with a watermelon skin fight and then a swim in the creek. Christmas on the farm holds many happy memories for me.

In strife

We got in trouble a few times during our years at Tanawha. I remember one time when Ian and I broke into an old shack about a mile away behind our farm. No one lived there but we thought it would be fun to see what was there. Well, we found some interesting things, one of them being a box of detonators, which we proceeded to throw around trying to get them to explode. Luckily for us none did. We were obviously seen because a couple of days later we had a visit from the police. They questioned us and I guess fortunately we told the truth. The police gave us a very stern warning and a ride in the police car, then they took us to the jail and told us that this is where we would end up if we continued to be "stupid." We learned a lesson.

Hitchhiking

One pastime which we occasionally had was to hitchhike to town, either Nambour, Maroochydore, Caloundra or sometimes Landsborough. Sometimes for fun we would hitch a ride and when a car pulled up we would run like mad and hide. This generally worked. There was one time when it did not though. I don't remember who I was with but we had a car with two older ladies in it pull up. We bolted and they eventually drove off after looking for us. Next thing we knew the police was driving up our road and proceeded to ask us plenty of questions. We were reprimanded and advised not to continue with this practise. I often wonder why these two old ladies reported us to the police. Maybe they were frustrated or something.

Nearly gone

Around the mid-fifties we started to get some of the early 22-wheeler trucks along the highway, as they moved goods up and down the state. On one occasion we were playing along the roadside near the front gate when I chased a ball onto the road and the next thing I heard was the terrible scream of tyres locked onto the bitumen. I froze and looked up straight into the grill of a great truck full of cattle. Fortunately it stopped, but only at the last second. This put the wind up in me for sure.

In the raw

We often went walking around the countryside and if it was hot we would end up swimming in one of the creeks or waterholes we came across. It was generally safe although I guess we did not consider snakes to be a threat. We lived with them in the country and therefore did not concern ourselves with them. On one occasion we decided to go swimming in a small billabong near Caloundra turnoff. There were four or five of us, girls included. We obviously were enjoying ourselves as we did not notice the two men who crept up and pinched all our clothes while we swam in the raw. We never noticed our clothes missing until we got out and could not find them. The two men were off in the distance laughing and they eventually told us where our clothes were. I suppose if this happened in today's society we may well have been at great risk, from "strange" people who are out there for more than just "fun.' Luckily for us this was merely a practical joke and was no more than that.

Rich for a day

Our family never had much in the way of money, but we nearly always had food and always had a roof over our heads, even though it may have been corrugated iron (which is great when it is raining). Because we didn't have much money, the local shops would allow our parents credit and we would book up essentials like bread, flour, sugar, tea, and rolled oats. The account would be paid for when we had enough money. One time some of us kids were walking along the side of the road and someone noticed something stuck in a tree. Upon investigation it was found to be a "tenner" or ten pound note. For us it was pure gold. We all raced to the shop about a mile away and bought an ice cream all round. The shopkeeper wanted us to pay the account but we would not let her keep the money, we took it home to show Mum and then we went back to the shop and paid off the account and brought some groceries. We all thought it was great to have this much money. This particular shopkeeper was Mrs. Frizzo who lived on the Landsborough side of Sippy Creek.

The old dodge truck

While we were still living at Tanawha, the only vehicle we had for years was the old Dodge truck. Dad would put a canvas canopy over a frame on the back and all of us kids would ride in the back. It was always great fun and there was always something happening. One time we had a swaggie doing some work for dad on the farm. I think he was an alcoholic and he obviously was running from some memories. However, one time when we were driving through Woolloongabba, with the truck full of kids and this swaggie bloke, the truck suddenly died and would not start again, so we all got off and pushed it through the five ways. Now the swaggie was a short little fellow and suddenly the truck fired into life and we all jumped back up onto the truck, all of us except the swaggie whose short legs were not quite long enough. It was the funniest thing watching him try and scramble fast enough to get back on board. He eventually was able to when a couple of the older boys grabbed his arms and dragged him over the tailgate.

Another time, when we had been to Caboolture to visit Uncle Bill and aunty Violet Adams, the truck broke down at the Kilcoy railway crossing on the north side of Caboolture. We spent the best part of a day broken down before we were able to head home to Tanawha. One time Dad was taking the truck back home from Buderim when one of the tierod ends snapped and he lost steering. Ever resourceful, Dad located an old tyre tube and put a figure of eight knot around the tie rod end with the tube and he finished the trip home.

Burning bush

Bush fires were a thing to be wary of in the bush, and they still are. One big fire we had at Tanawha burnt for several days and the only way we could control it was by back burning. To do any good with a back burn you need to be able to start it early and get it going well so that it ends up as big as the fire you want to stop. If this is not done then the main fire will overcome the back burn and just jump over it. I have seen this happen several times. On this occasion at Tanawha we started the back burn along our road from the highway to the house and when the two fires met about half a mile from where we started the back burn, there were several quite large explosions, which we found to be trees which had literally exploded when the fires met. We were involved in two other large fires many years later both at Hughenden. One was on the western side and burnt out several large properties before eventually being controlled, again only through back burning. During this particular fire a new implement was used for lighting some of the back burn. A welder in Hughenden, Ken Doyle, had manufactured a plough with the capability of having a flame thrower attached. This was dragged behind a grader and it lit the grass at the same time a firebreak was made. The grader had to keep moving at a good speed otherwise it would have been burnt. This contraption was quite successful and is still used today in the outback. One property had a lot of their country burnt and it is amazing what people will do to try and save their livelihood. One lady literally tied herself to the steering wheel of her water truck so she would not fall out if she went to sleep while carting water to the firefighters. I think she was behind the wheel for about three day's non-stop as was one of her kids who was about 9-10 years old. She drove a Land Cruiser and supplied food and drink to those involved in the firefighting. I guess there were other people who put themselves in the same situation. I know this woman personally as I was there when the fire happened and I assisted with the firefighting.

Sometime around 1975 or 1976, another fire involved some good friends of ours who owned a cattle property at Torrens Creek. Heather received a phone call from a tearful Daphne Pearce at about 5:30pm one Friday evening.

As their property was surrounded by fire and it looked like they may be burnt out, Heather told Daphne that we would all be down as soon as I knocked off work at 6pm. Heather packed some old clothes for me and all the kids and we set off. Torrens Creek is about 60 miles from Hughenden. When we arrived, our families gathered for prayer. There were about 8 Pearce kids plus mum and dad, Heather and I and our three kids plus our Aboriginal foster daughter Elizabeth. We are all Seventh-day Adventists and this was now our Sabbath. What should we do? We do not normally work on the Sabbath but Jesus gave us the example of the lost sheep. We did not want the property burnt out, nor any of their cattle burnt. We asked the Lord for assistance with the fire and our prayers were answered that night. We started back burning from the fence line of one of the paddocks which was about 10-15 thousand acres, and sent the fire back towards itself. One of the vehicles was used to carry water for firefighting and also to bring food and drink for all the workers. Daphne kept up a supply of good food as we kept burning all night and come Sabbath morning it was time to see what damage had been done. We never had a fire in the paddock where we back burnt from and only one tree had burnt and fallen across the fence line into this paddock. No stock was hurt or lost that night, no person was injured, and this paddock was saved from any damage. Surely God does answer prayers, and I am sure He with his angels also fought bushfires that night.

Farm work

We generally worked hard on the farm although we did have fun as well. We had to make our own fun though as most bush kids did and still do. We split fence posts by hand, cut trees down with our axes, and cut logs in half using a crosscut saw and an axe. There were not many chainsaws around, although Merv Ross had a couple. One was a small Blue Streak and the other was a massive two man Denarm with an around 6-foot-long blade that was a struggle to carry around the bush. Sam Tomlinson was once cut badly with a chain saw and he had to have 800 stitches in his stomach area where he was ripped open. Dad operated a sawmill for some time which cut house timber and case timber on the farm. Uncle Dave Gould worked and lived with us for a short time after he married Dad's sister May who died from asthma sometime in the late sixties. Uncle Dave was working on the saw bench one time when he got caught by the saw and cut a couple of fingers off. Dad loaded him into the old Dodge truck and they set off to meet the ambulance from Nambour. The old truck must have been flying as they got three parts of the way into Nambour before meeting the ambulance. The fingers were never found.

Fertiliser

Brother John once cut off the top of one of his fingers and we had a burial service for it just under the edge of the front of the house. We planted a bracken fern on top of it which grew very well.

Early start

In about 1963, Mum and Dad moved to Caboolture so that Dad could find work nearby, and also because we kids were growing older and we needed better schooling and job opportunities. For the first time in about 12 years, we had electricity. It was marvellous to be able to flick a switch and have the light come on. We rented a house on Toorbul road at first. I remember one morning being woken up and as was my usual response I wandered outside to cut some wood for the fire so that we could boil the billy. I was promptly reminded that it was only 3:30am as Dad was leaving for work. I think he was going to Rathdowney to do some scrub felling.

Unseen eclipse

Another early morning episode revolved around a total eclipse of the moon. We were at Tanawha at the time, I was about 10 and we pestered Dad to wake us kids up so we could see the eclipse which would occur at about 2:00am. Dad apparently woke us all up but I don't think any of us can remember seeing the eclipse.

Caboolture

We eventually moved from the house on Toorbul road to another property further out on the same road but about a mile off the road. This property was a chook farm and was owned by Mr. & Mrs. Mollenhauer. The rent was quite cheap, at I think about 4 dollars per week. It was at this time that I met Heather Mollenhauer and we went on our first outing by ourselves in June 1963 when we went to the Caboolture show. We eventually got married on August 23, 1965.

Rathdowney

After leaving Caboolture in about 1964, the family moved to Rathdowney and lived in an old weather board house at the head of Running Creek. This was and still is a beautiful place. Dad did quite a lot of scrub felling in this area. We also lived in a house at Palen Creek, not far from the prison farm. This too was a pretty place to live. While here we were able to do a lot of bush walking in the thick scrub and heavy forest around the Mount Barney area. Dad was offered a bigger house at one time about 3 miles up the road. The date was fixed for us to move in when the owner moved out. We waited until the day after and then loaded all our furniture onto the Dodge and away we went only to find the house still full of the owner's furniture. She was not a happy lady when she got home and saw that we had moved in. We were promptly evicted without even spending one night in the house, so we moved back into the old cottage again. We did have a great feed of her grapes though. It was while we were living here that I got serious about Heather and eventually moved out and lived on the job with the railway. But while at Palen Creek, we had a few different experiences. While swimming down the creek in the raw, Keith and Betty who were on a dairy farm at Christmas Creek, visited and stole our clothes. We were able to find a tree with large leaves and made ourselves some "natural" clothes and proceeded home in this attire. One time we were shooting birds with a shotgun and Cecil decided that he would have a go, so he lined up some birds which were in a tree that we were directly under, so he had to look straight up to shoot them. This was not a good idea with a double barrel shot gun. Poor Cecil ended up flat on his back and was covered in bird feathers. He was sore for a week.

Leaving home

Just after I left home, I purchased my first car, a second hand Austin A40. It went like a beauty, it was grey with leather upholstery. On a visit home at Christmas time it was decided that we will visit Keith and Betty so off we went. I was a bit tired and there were 11 of us in the A40, so to keep me awake the rest decided to sing some songs. The first one they sang was "Silent Night" which promptly put me to sleep. Luckily we only had a few miles to go with so many people in the car. The poor old A40 was involved in a crash at the valley 5 ways. There was a cop on points duty who waved me through, but unfortunately there was also an old lady in a Rolls Royce on the same corner, she was pulled up by the cop but did not think that she should have to wait for an inferior vehicle like mine so she ran a red light as it were and we collided. I was able to drive home but the Rolls was immobilised as the radiator was damaged and the guard was pushed back onto the wheel and could not be moved. Heather's dad and I did some panel beating on the A40 and she was okay. We had a lot of fun living in this area. It still holds fond memories for me.

A new beginning

Heather and I got engaged in February 1964 and we married on Heather's birthday in August 1965. Her parents were not impressed by this, especially her mother. I think her dad accepted that we would do okay but her mother did not like me at all. I think she was jealous and she would often call me to come and massage her chest and back. I remember one time Heather's dad came out to the Delaneys Creek dance hall to get me so that I could help her mum with her asthma attack. She asked me to massage her chest to help relieve the breathing, and I think this was a ploy to have me play with her breasts, as she seemed to enjoy these times. One time, she was in bed for three or four weeks with asthma after she realised that I was visiting Heather and that I was not particularly interested in her or her body. My relationship with Heather's mum has always been strained. She has told some terrible stories about me and Heather, one in particular was when Heather was looking after Aunty Mable and her boys when Uncle Norman was sick just before he died. Heather's mum started a story that Heather was pregnant and had been taken away by the Salvation Army to have a baby, which was to be adopted out. We only found out about this because one of my aunties was in the Salvation Army in Caboolture and asked me about this. I was as shocked as my Aunty Violet. We have fortunately overcome all the problems associated with such a weird lady, who by the way delves a little into witchcraft and voodoo. She once sent me a voodoo doll full of pins. I guess it was meant to scare me but I figured it was a waste of a good doll and lots of pins. We still do what we can for her but it never satisfies nor makes her any more a favourite. She is very difficult to satisfy regardless of what happens, but I have remained married to her daughter and tried to be a good son-in-law.

Heather and I have had a pretty good married life. We have not had any fierce fights as some do. Sure, we had disagreements and our ups and downs but nothing big enough to make us want to leave each other. Most of our disagreements have been over work and perhaps the farm with regard to how it should operate and how much time it should take up. Work did take up a lot of my time and as a result Heather was often left for long periods of time with the kids, sometimes even at important times. She often had to wait for me to finish the job I was on and this would sometimes take several hours. But despite all this our married life up to now has been worthwhile and rewarding.

First house and sick kids

Our first home was purchased in 1968 in Caboolture, Dances Road. It was a small four-room weatherboard cottage with no ceiling or linings. There was a tin car shed as well. The 2-acre property was about three kilometres from town. It was beside the railway line just north of Caboolture. We paid $1,800.00 for the place and had to borrow the $200.00 deposit from the bank. You couldn't do that in 2005. We spent some extra money over three years of doing work on the house. We bought one sheet of material at a time and eventually lined and ceiled it. I painted the shed silver and started a garden which had vegetables and also trees for shade and beauty around the place. We built a chook pen with chooks and some ducks. The ducks were left on our front steps one day by Rob Duncalfe. Alan adopted the ducks (or they adopted him) and they would follow him everywhere. There were several of them. Our children spent their first few years in this house. Rose started kindergarten and school while we were here. Alan broke a leg at this house one time, he just sat down and it cracked the bone. He was in plaster for several weeks and loved going outside in the rain with the plaster, which did not last long in these conditions. Nigel was very ill while we lived here. He suffered from pyloric stenosis which affected him quite badly. At three months old, he went below his birth weight overnight. We thought he was going to die. I took him to Redcliffe hospital, then he was transferred to Brisbane and then into a special care hospice where he had multiple tests to try and find out the problem. The doctors told Heather and me to have a few days away, but to keep in touch. They thought he would not pull through. We went to Tenterfield and across to Lismore and had a look around for about 5 days. Pat & Lil were with us as were our kids. We arrived home and Nigel was much improved. At this point we were advised that it would be wise to move to a drier climate which would help Nigel get better. We had to feed him with a product called "Nestargel" which made everything he ate as thick as glue, so that he could not vomit it out. We moved to Cloncurry in June 1973.

Death in the family

Heather's dad was killed while we were living here. I had been in the ambulance as a collector for about a year in Brisbane since I started on July 9th, 1969. I was doing a first aid course at Caboolture Ambulance when the superintendent Ian Mackay asked me if I was interested in working at Caboolture. I was travelling to Brisbane daily at this time. I took the job as a bearer/ collector at Caboolture and started on June 8, 1970. I was working this day as an ambulance officer. I had an elders' meeting to attend at Nambour church at 6 pm that night so as soon as I knocked off at 4pm we took off to Nambour. Heather and the kids went to visit Aunty Mable and I went to the meeting. At about 6:45 the police arrived where we had the meeting and informed me that there had been an accident involving Heather's dad, William Mollenhauer. I left the meeting, picked up the family and went back to

Caboolture. We were told that Dad had been killed in a train accident at Narangba, he died instantly of a literal broken heart. The impact ruptured his heart. His best friend William De-knock was also seriously injured in the same accident and died the next day. Had I not started work at Caboolture on that day I would have been on the train too, and in the same carriage as Dad. I also think my life would have changed had I been in town at the time of the accident. I would have been called into duty and gone to the crash scene. I do not know how I would have handled this particular job. Shirley's ex-husband Eric Morgan was there as he worked in the railway. During the accident there was a lot of activity going on and Eric spotted someone taking off with Dad's work port, then when he was questioned about it, his response was "The bloke is dead he won't need it." You gotta be quick. This was greatly upsetting for Heather as she was very close to her dad, but our support and her faith allowed her to move on.

Train crash

Another accident which had a big impact on us happened one night in November 1971 when the rail bridge near our place was washed away in a flood and a goods train was washed off the line. We heard the crash and straightaway rang emergency to report it. Fortunately, no one was injured. But it took several days before the line was repaired. This accident brought back all the emotions from when Dad was killed. I understand that the crew on the train which ran into the back of Dad's train were drunk.

Little boy lost

While living in this house, there was one time when we lost Alan who was about three years old at the time. Heather rang me all upset that she could not find the boy. I set off toward home and would you believe that I found him sitting on the side of a small gully, fishing for tadpoles? This was on

Dances Road about half a mile from the house. We paid for this house when Dad's will was settled and Shirley bought out Heather's share of the George Street house he owned. We were taken for a ride by Shirley and the others as the house was not correctly valued. We were in this house for about 4 years and realised a tidy profit when we sold it. It was a great start for us and we have fond memories of our time there. Family members used to visit us and helped us clear the block and fix the fences.

Mother-in-law

Heather's mother was with us for a short time after Dad was killed. We put her in the only other bedroom we had and the kids shared our room and the lounge. While she was there, Heather had an experience with the devil. As I said earlier, Heather's mother delved into spiritism and one time she was not well and Heather tried to get into the bedroom but she could not get past the doorway. She realised what was happening and shouted, "Satan get out of our house and do not come back!" The Lord heard and Satan was evicted. Heather was then able to walk through the doorway. There was no door on the room, only a curtain.

Blown away

On Christmas Eve in 1974, we were living and working at Hughenden. Pat & Lil were also there, and we decided that we would clamp down at Porcupine Gorge for the night and spend Christmas day in the gorge, which is about 60 kilometres north of Hughenden. This was the Christmas Eve when Tracy destroyed Darwin. Pat and I had finished setting up camp and we decided to go for a walk and check out the fishing and swimming prospects. We came across a small rock pool where several bony bream were caught. We scooped them up and put them on a stick to take home. Well, what a surprise everyone got, they reckoned we had met up with some other people who had given them to us. It took a lot of talking to convince them that we had actually caught these by ourselves.

Career moves

We moved several times before and during my ambulance career. The first place we lived after getting married (we did not live together before then) was a small house near Lake Kurwongba at Petrie. We then moved to a house beside the railway line at Lawnton, and it was during these times that I was working as a truck driver in Brisbane while also working at the Albion flour mill. We then moved to Caboolture where we bought a home at Dances Road. This was the time when I joined the Ambulance. We moved from Caboolture to Cloncurry in 1973 and what a move that was, we purchased a two-ton Bedford truck and with the help of Ted Bakke we built sides for it so that we could move ourselves. We also built a 6X4 trailer to carry some of our stuff. I still have the trailer until now. We loaded everything we wanted and set off. Phillip came with us as a relief driver. I was driving the Bedford with a caravan behind and Heather and Phillip were in our falcon with the trailer. I got to Jackass creek just south of Gympie and met with a semi on the bridge. His rear view mirror opened up the side of our caravan like a pair of scissors. Stuff was spread all over the road. Heather, who was a few minutes behind me, came around the corner and recognised the kids' clothes and toys on the road. We managed to get everything back into the van and set off for Maryborough where we bought another old van and continued our trip. When we left Rockhampton we decided that we would meet near Marlborough at a park for lunch. I headed off first with two of the kids then Heather and Phillip with one of the kids followed. We got separated at some roadworks. I kept going to the park at Marlborough and had only arrived there for a few minutes when Heather turned up out of a side road.

She had been diverted at the roadworks and travelled through several outback roads through some properties. The Lord led them to the park, for sure. On the road between Julia Creek and Cloncurry I was driving the falcon and trailer when the axle of the trailer broke in two. I borrowed some No. 8 wire from a property fence and tied the axle back into place and continued with our trip to Cloncurry. We eventually arrived there after about a week on the road. We sent Phillip home by bus after a few days.

We spent just a year at Cloncurry and then moved to Hughenden, where we purchased our second home. We stayed there for 5 years and then moved to Thursday Island for 15 months and then to Winton for three years. The next move was to Stanthorpe where we lived for 17 years. I retired from Stanthorpe on July 9, 2000, then we moved full time to the farm.

Moving can be interesting and several things stand out for me. When we moved from Cloncurry to Hughenden, the furniture went by train and a couple of boxes went missing during this trip and after many years we would suddenly discover something else that was in those boxes. When we transferred to Thursday Island, the removal truck came from Townsville and had trouble locating our house. Everyone they asked would not tell the driver our address. Obviously, the people of the town did not want us to shift. We had been there 5 years and loved the place, but my promotion to superintendent meant that we had to move. Our furniture was moved from Townsville to Thursday Island by boat. I am thankful that the QATB paid for this move, though they did not pay to move me back to Winton after my time on Thursday Island. They then paid for me to move from Winton to Stanthorpe. We moved ourselves from Stanthorpe to the farm over a period of several months when we had finally set the date for my retirement. We would move a Ute full of stuff every time we had days off and eventually had it all moved.

There are many, many stories I could tell but this is a taste of the complexity of the work I was involved in over 30 years of my career in the Queensland Ambulance Service. I enjoyed my time in the Service although there were many unpleasant administration changes to add to the trauma of the work. But if I had to do it all over again I would not change anything at all.

We had purchased a small 75-acre lifestyle block in 1980 and by 2000 it was time to retire. I had been diagnosed with the propensity to become diabetic in November 1999 and the advice from my doctor was to retire. I told her that me and my wife had already decided to retire at age 55. I did some relief work for a few years after but I did retire from full-time work on July 9, 2000. I fully gave up ambulance work in August 2004.

On July 9, 2000, we moved the last of our belongings and ourselves over to "the farm" at Mount Binga, near Blackbutt. We had just finished having a nice home built, and we were able to move straight in. What a feeling it was to wake up on July 10 and not have to put my uniform on. I assumed the position of "boss" on the farm but I was often reminded that I was still married to Heather. It was wonderful to know that now I would not have deadlines to meet with reporting, I would not have to be so giving of myself to other people as I had done for the past 30 years. It does and did take its toll on me as I found out over the years. I did get a lot of satisfaction from my public duty as an ambo but the price was paid. I now had diabetes from the lifestyle I had lived for so many years, not getting enough exercise, having to eat broken meals and eating the wrong foods, because when out after hours one could only obtain fast food and this would sit on the stomach and turn to fat, which is not good for the body. I suppose one could have worked harder at keeping fit and looking after the body, but it is very difficult when all your energy is spent after a hectic day's work, there was no energy left for exercise. I only needed rest. During my career, I did find that I could have a nana-nap when needed. I would sit in the lounge with a metal plate on the floor and a teaspoon in my hand, completely relax and the spoon would drop when I nodded off. I found that this would be equivalent to a good four hours of sleep. I had to do this regularly as there were many times when I was sleep-deprived, having been woken from sleep up to five times a night, sometimes to go on a trip which would take several hours of driving and then treating patients. In the smaller station there was no relief but the patients still required service, and we had to serve with a smile.

Snakes alive

On February 4, 2004, I was chasing a cow of ours back out of the neighbour's paddock. I was in our place walking around the boundary which my granddaughter had mowed only a couple of days earlier. It was a six-foot-wide strip. I had on a pair of shorts, a t-shirt, a pair of elastic side boots, and a stockwhip over my shoulder. I felt something hit my left ankle with such force that I stumbled and almost fell over. Looking down, I saw a large eastern brown snake beside my ankle together with a red-striped frog. It seemed that the snake had struck at me on the ankle, but my guardian angel (who I am sure has a sense of humour) must have put the frog in the snake's mouth just before he hit me. We pray daily for the Lord to protect us and he did that day. I was about 300 meters from home, and if the snake had bitten me I was in trouble. The reptile was a good six feet long, and I had little to treat myself. I should also mention that the snake does not eat red-striped frogs. I got home but I was somewhat shaken up, knowing what could have happened. I thank God for his goodness and protection.

Family increase

I did some interesting things on the farm. There were several times when we had to pull a calf out when the mother cow had problems. One of them involved a rope around the back legs of the calf. Brother John and I were pulling with all our weight until the calf was delivered and both were okay. Another one involved our four-wheel drive and a rope, again the rope was around the legs and we pulled until the calf was born, both were well this time also. Another time, we had an older cow struggling to give birth and with a lot of help the calf finally emerged unscathed, but the mother was not doing so well. I had to insert my arm into the cow to ensure the afterbirth was delivered. That was a different thing to do, but it worked.

Playtime

Occasionally, we did have time for fun and games. Every year, our family would have a family reunion. All my siblings and their children would attend and we would total sometimes up to 60 or so people. The families would bring tents, caravans, and other bedding and sleep wherever they could. Over the years, I built some accommodation, and when we built the new house, we then had the cottage which at various times slept up to 30 people on wall to wall mattresses. I also built a good campfire area and a nine-hole bush golf course. The farm was a good place to hold family and church gatherings all year round. Heather and I would often lie in bed and watch a heap of very amateur golfers giggle and hit around the outside of the house garden. It was great fun. We would also sometimes play Frisbee golf with some hoops I made to get the Frisbee through. We had cricket matches, football games, badminton, and any other games people would organise. At various times, we would have church picnics and pathfinder camps on the farm, which were thoroughly enjoyed by all who attended. Even though we have not been on the farm for several years, the family and church folk still comment on the good times they had out there.

Church

My whole life from when I was about 19 years old has been connected to our church, the Seventh-day Adventist Church. Both Heather and I have been involved in church life, in many churches across the state, with me being elder, treasurer, SS Super, pathfinder leader, deacon, youth leader at various churches over the years. Heather has also held several positions. She was deaconess, assist pathfinder, and children's leader. I have been a lay preacher in the church since 1965. We have both been really blessed by our membership in this church and even more blessed with our relationship with our Lord and Saviour, Jesus Christ. We are ready and are waiting for His return in the clouds of glory.

Two events which did have an impact on our lives was our long-term involvement with our foster children. Over the years, we had about 30 or more children we looked after for more than a couple of months. But two of our foster tribe were long-term. One was Elizabeth Miller from Weipa, a full blood Aboriginal who came to us while we were in Hughenden. She was about eight at the time and she was a typical Aboriginal piccaninny. She fitted into our family quite well and was accepted by our children, but she did have some traits which were typically Aboriginal, like sitting in the dirt poking a fire and talking to herself. Elizabeth did have some racial prejudice against her at school, but our kids would stick up for her. She came from a family of seven kids, her parents were both alcoholics and her dad was a singer and guitar player. She remained with us for several years until she got homesick and said she wanted to go home to Weipa. We took her to Townsville where the Department of Child Services took her back home. We have remained in touch all the time since, and we have been able to see her a few times at Weipa.

She now lives with her partner Jonothan in Cairns, and she had two girls who have had several children between them. We are proud that they call us Mum and Dad and Grandma and Grandad.

The other foster child we had has been with us since he was a young man from India. His name was Devadenam Pasmerella and he is now in his mid-forties. He came from a village outside Hyderabad in India. He was about five years old when we first started putting him through school. His dad could not work and his mother was not well, they were very poor. We accepted him through an agency of our church called Asian Aid. He was taken from his village to our orphanage to get his education, with the permission of his parents. After state school, he applied and received a scholarship to high school where he graduated with very high marks. He wanted to go to university and his marks were good enough. He entered a competition through the Indian Government to win a scholarship to study biochemistry. There were 55,000 applicants who sat the exam and he received the second highest pass mark for the entrance exam and won a full scholarship to uni. We lost touch for many years but one day 17 years ago he contacted us. He told me that he has met several Prime Ministers of Australia, had been to many trade missions and met several other politicians. Once he got introduced to them he would always ask if they knew Victor Torrens in Australia. After uni, he became a Cancer Research Scientist and was involved in several cancer cures for the American Army, which are not yet open to the public domain. He was recently married to Grace. His mother at this time is not well and is undergoing therapy for throat cancer. We hope to be able to meet each other soon, although we talk regularly on *WhatsApp* and *Skype*.

The following are memories of jobs I have been involved in throughout my ambulance career. My career spanned from June 9, 1969, until November 2004. I will endeavour to write these stories without identifying any of the patients involved. They are all true to my memory.

There is much more one could write, but there has to be a cut- off point into how much one puts on paper. My memory has a lot more information and I am happy to talk about it to anyone who will listen. Perhaps even another volume.

30 Seconds with a Paramedic

Victor Torrens

SUICIDE ATTEMPT

One of the first memorable jobs I had was when I received a call regarding a woman who had threatened to cut her throat with a kitchen knife. I was very new as a paramedic at this time, having only been appointed for some months. This day, I was working with Joe Shears, who had many years of service. I was all fired up and ready to go when Joe decided that it was time for him to have a smoke. He calmly rolled one and sat there smoking. Perhaps I looked concerned because Joe told me, "What is the hurry, we cannot do anything until she does cut her throat." We eventually took off to the house, which was a few miles out of Caboolture. Upon arrival, we were met by the frantic husband who told us that his wife had "gone bush" and he had no idea where she was. With some help from the local police, we found her sitting on a log in the bush. She was quite agitated and very angry. She did not have the knife then and did not appear to be hurt. We talked her into coming with us in the ambulance for treatment at the hospital. We took off to the RBH, and I was looking after her in the back of the unit. On the way she was trying to take some bex powders (painkillers), which were toxic in large doses. She had them down her blouse, and me being a gentleman, I did not want to go fishing for them in that place. I decided to just restrain her arms to keep her from getting the powders. She then bit me on the forearm which bled and caused me some pain. We eventually got her to RBH with no further incidents and about two weeks later she called into the ambulance station. She visited to apologise for her behaviour and for biting me. She was on medication and was quite normal.

PLAYING CHICKEN AFTER A MOUNTAIN ACCIDENT

I received a call one afternoon at about 3pm to attend to an incident on Mt. Tibrogargan at Glasshouse. I was with another ambo and two police officers. The incident involved a young man falling down the side of the mountain while attempting to climb to the top. His mate saw him fall and went for help. We however had a problem because he did not mark or remember where his mate fell. The Glasshouse Mountains rescue group were sent to find him. By the time we arrived at a designated point about a third of the way up the mountain, it was night time and quite dark. We had carried our equipment including a stretcher with us. One of the policemen said he needed some sleep as he had worked most of the previous night. He was also scared that he might fall off the ledge if he went to sleep. We solved this problem by tying a rope around his leg and wrapping the rope around a big boulder. He was able to catch a few hours of sleep like this. The ledge was about 8 feet wide and maybe 10 feet long. At around midnight, the patient was found and brought to us. Both his legs were broken and he had injuries on his head and other parts of his body. After carrying him down to the ambulance, I was given the job of taking him to RBH for treatment. He was in a bad way by this time.

While I was on the highway on the way to Brisbane, two men in a twin spinner Ford started playing chicken with me. It is advisable to maintain a constant speed when transporting an injured patient. These men were passing me and then slowing right down which caused me to shift between having to brake and accelerate to the detriment of the patient. I got on the radio to tell the police about my problem. They advised me to meet them at Chermside. When we got to Chermside, the traffic lights were red, so with my lights and siren I was able to run the light, and so did the two in the Ford, straight into the arms of the waiting police. The patient did survive and returned home to England after treatment. I do not know what happened to the two in the twin spinner Ford.

SOME HANKY PANKY

Another job I was in involved concerned four young people in a motor accident. Two girls and two blokes. The story was that the two girls were travelling from Cairns to Brisbane and picked the two blokes, who were soldiers, up near Mackay. Obviously some close connections were formed in the days of the trip. This was about 1970 or 1971. The driver lost control of the car near Burpengary and it rolled several times and ended up in a large heap of wooden bridge girders. All of the patients had broken bones and other injuries. They were all in different stages of undress, with very little clothes on at all. (The mind wonders what was going on in the car.) I placed one girl and one man in my ambulance and set off for Brisbane hospital. The girl had a broken leg and head injuries among other injuries, fortunately none of them life-threatening. The man had both his legs broken among other injuries. I was the only officer in the car in this situation, we did not have all the backup they now have. I turned the rear view mirror down to watch the patients as I drove. Both patients had been splinted and bandaged as required for the trip. After a few minutes on the road, I looked in the mirror and both patients were on the one stretcher. Quite obviously, they wanted to finish what had been started in the car before the accident.

What should I do? I contacted base and requested another car to take one of the patients. Both patients were upset that they were to be split up. I felt that it was bad enough to tell the girl's parents about the accident, without having to tell them that she may also be pregnant by the time she got out of the hospital.

BEHEADED

This happened while I was still new to the job in Caboolture. Four young fellows were hitchhiking from Woodford to Brisbane and were picked up by a young chap in a Ute. One got in the front and the three others got in the back of the Ute. When they got to Caboolture, the driver decided to pass a car on the left side. As they rapidly went past the ambulance station, there was a row of Camphor Laurel trees right down the street. One of the trees had a low hanging branch which missed the roof of the Ute but did not miss the three in the back. Each one of them literally had his head knocked off and busted open like ripe watermelons. We heard the Ute and then the screams of the passenger in the front as it sped off further down the main street, past the police station. After a few minutes, the Ute screeched to a stop in front of the ambulance. At this stage we were unaware of what had happened. The driver raced straight through the centre and down into some long grass in the park behind us. The passenger told us what he thought had happened. We looked in the back of the Ute and found three headless bodies. We then had the grisly task of finding the heads and what remained of them. We collected them in plastic bags, then the police came and arrested the driver who was subsequently charged with DUI as he was on alcohol and drugs at the time. I am still amazed that young people today think that they are invincible when they're in a vehicle.

Victor Torrens

LOST BABY AT ACCIDENT

I received a call one late Saturday night regarding an accident at Burpengary. A car had run headfirst into the side rails on a bridge. When we got there, the two occupants were unconscious with multiple injuries. First aid was promptly given and they were off to Redcliffe hospital. While at the hospital, one of the nurses recognised the couple and asked us where their 3-month-old baby was. We had no idea, so we went back to the scene to look around further. By this time the car had been taken to a garage, so we searched the car first but it was no good. We then went back to the creek with assistance. We searched a large area of water and the creek bank to no avail. The police went to check on the parents of the patients and they came back and told us the baby was with a baby sitter. That was a great relief.

JUST NOT FAIR

Another call we got was one of the many very sad calls we had received. This call came on a Sunday afternoon. The report was a bad motor accident. We responded on the old Gympie road near Elimbah, north of Caboolture. What a mess it was when we arrived. We were looking at two cars embedded into each other and several bodies strewn around a fairly large area. Our examination found only one person alive who was about 60 years old. There were five dead persons. They turned out to be a father, mother, and three children. What transpired was the lone driver who was heading home after a day at his local bowls club approached a long left hand corner while he was on the wrong side of the road, and the other car was apparently heading home after a family picnic. The father who was driving appeared to have moved over to the wrong side of the road to avoid an accident, and at the same time the lone driver went back to his side of the road and they ran head long into each other. He was not injured in any way. He was eventually charged with drunk driving. The father was blamed for the accident as he was on the wrong side of the road at point of impact, regardless of the testimonies of several witnesses of the accident. Sometimes the law is an ass.

WRONG SIDE OF THE ROAD

Sometimes we had to drive at high speeds and sometimes even on the wrong side of the road. This may explain why I now drive more sedately than other road users. One such case involved an elderly patient playing bowls at Glass House on a Sunday afternoon. He simultaneously suffered a stroke and cardiac arrest. He was very sick. I stabilised him and while someone kept an eye on him in the back, I headed off to Redcliffe Hospital while driving at a high speed. There was bumper to bumper traffic from Caloundra turnoff all the way to Brisbane. I was driving on the wrong side of the road with very little oncoming traffic. Near the Bribie Island turnoff, I noticed a car coming towards me. It appeared to not see me even though I had the lights and the siren on. Eventually, after I searched for a way out, the driver did spot me then headed onto the verge, which luckily was quite wide. I was quite shook up by this time. I got my patient to the hospital and he did survive albeit in a reduced capacity. After a few hours back at the station we had a lady call in about her young daughter who received some nasty cuts on her buttocks when she came down a slippery slide in the park. While dressing her daughters wounds this lady proceeded to tell us about the scare she got when an ambulance was driving down the wrong side of the highway at a very high speed. I did not enlighten her that I was the driver.

NAILED BY THE HEAD

We got a call about someone impaled onto a lump of 3x2. We headed down to Deception Bay and upon arrival we found a 10 year old boy literally nailed to an 8-foot-long piece of 3X2. He was playing tiggy with his mates when he ran around the corner of the house and into this piece of timber which had a 4-inch nail through it. We did not attempt to take the nail out so we drove him to the hospital with the timber supported by two people in the back of the ambulance. The nail was removed under anaesthetic. I guess the boy had a story to tell.

BLOWN UP

It was Saturday afternoon, a car raced to a screeching stop in front of the station and two men jumped out. One was literally covered in blood (not a pretty sight and he had completely lost his left hand). We endeavoured to stem the bleeding and we wrapped the injury. We also called a local doctor in to set up an infusion on this patient. After this we took him to Redcliffe Hospital, which by the way my father helped build. While there he was assessed and then we transported him to RBH for further treatment.

He told us what happened when he first arrived at the station in bad shock while suffering severe injuries. He claimed that his mate had driven him to Beachmere to see his girlfriend (who happened to be married). On their way back they passed the husband's car going home. When he passed them he apparently dropped something out of his car. When the Casanova bent down to pick it up, the thing exploded, blowing his hand right off and straight into his face. He was a real mess. We had called the police when he arrived and told us this story. This guy told the exact same story to the police. When we arrived at Redcliffe, we were met by a couple of detectives, who also got the same story and again at RBH he told the same exact story to other detectives. This person by the way was a retired boxer and a little "punch drunk."

About three weeks later, he visited the station again, and his stump was almost completely healed. He had decided that he better tell us the real story. We listened intently. It seems that he was in fact blowing fish with his mate. He was working for a big contractor doing sewerage works for the local council. He had stolen some gelignite, fuses and detonators from his boss, and not knowing much about it he went to show his mate what to do. What happened was that the fuse he had stolen was faulty and had some spaces in the powder, which meant that the spark would jump up to three inches once it was lit. He obviously lit one and was counting the mandatory 3 seconds before throwing it into the water, when it suddenly exploded and blew his hand into his face. He recovered well and was given his job back. Remember that these two men made this story up while racing at high speed for about 12 kilometres to get assistance for a serious injury. It's amazing how the mind of people can work against all odds.

IT IS NOT A GOOD IDEA TO SMOKE

A Spanish man who was about 63 years old was booked to travel by plane back to Spain where he had not visited since he was a teenager. He was really looking forward to this trip, about 8 weeks from then, with his wife.

They owned a pineapple farm north of Caboolture. He had just finished spraying his crop using a 5000 gallon tank and decided to wash it out, using petrol which was the standard back then. After washing the inside of the tank, the man decided that it was time for a smoke. He sat on a 20-litre fuel drum straight under the opening of the tank, then rolled and lit his cigarette. Obviously, there was quite an explosion as the fuel fumes ignited. Fortunately for this chap, he was blown directly upward by the explosion and went straight through the opening and he landed about 60 feet away. When I got there he was in a bad way with about 85% of his body burnt. He refused any pain relief as he said he was not in pain. I wrapped him in a couple of wet sheets and took off to the burns unit at RBH about 30 minutes away. After six weeks I got a visit at work from this chap and he was walking unaided and seemed to be in good health. He had healed enough for the doctors to give him permission to travel home for their holiday. I consider this was made possible by this man's positive attitude and drive to go on the trip.

SUNBATHING IN THE RAW IS NOT GOOD

One Sunday afternoon, we heard the cas room bell and had a young lady who was about 18 or 19 years old. She was in a bad way suffering from severe sunburn. At the time we had a mixture for treating sunburn made up by our local chemist (it was very good). This girl had spent the day sunbathing in the nude on Bribie Island, and she was really badly burnt. As was our practice in these situations, two officers always treated the patients for the security of the patient and also for our own safety. Even back then in 1972, one had to be careful of any improprieties. We started to treat this girl and we literally had to paint her from head to toe with the fluid. She therefore had to have no clothes on, although I reckon she was used to that. At one point during the treatment we heard a knock on the door and before we could reach the door to see who it was it was pushed open by an elderly lady. She took one look at the situation, said something like "Oh-Oh," and promptly left. We never did find out what she wanted, or even what she thought was going on. The girl ended up in the burns unit at RBH for a few days to recover.

LOST PATIENT FOUND

One time, I received a call at about midmorning regarding a car accident near the Bribie Island turnoff on the Bruce Highway. When we got there we could not find any patients, and after a search of the area, we decided that the driver had probably shot through and had gotten a lift home with someone. Back at the station, while having lunch, we got a call about a person suffering shock at a house near Bribie turnoff. We responded and upon arrival found a 50-odd-year-old male collapsed on the floor. He was in deep shock and obviously had internal injuries. We had to rush him to RBH for treatment. It appears that he was the driver of the earlier crash, and these kind people had taken him to their house, gave him a cuppa, then looked after him and eventually gave him lunch. After he had eaten lunch he promptly collapsed and then we were called. It never did and still does not make sense for people to be taken from the scene of an accident before being checked out by people who know what to look for.

Victor Torrens

BABY REVIVED

I got a call to respond to a baby who was not breathing. It was near the highway at Burpengary. When I arrived, the mother was frantic, she handed me her baby who was only a few months old. I commenced CPR, and we had no electronic devices to help us back then so it was only me, God and what knowledge I had that worked that day. After about 15 minutes, I had restarted the baby's heart and she was breathing again. No one knows how great that feeling is unless you have had the personal experience. I gave the baby back to her mum and with my lights and siren on I hightailed it to Redcliffe Hospital which was about 12 minutes away. As far as I know the girl suffered no after effects from her ordeal. This case was apparently SIDS, which was reversed. I thank God daily for his assistance and for giving me strength as I worked as a paramedic.

SPIRITUALISM IN THE FAMILY

For many years, Heather's mother has been involved in some form of spirit worship. She has always claimed to be a Christian, but I am never sure of this. We have had several incidents of witnessing some sort of satanic influence with her. Not long after her husband, Heather's father, was killed in a train crash at Narangba in 1970, she fell ill and Heather and I decided that she would look after her mum in our cottage, rather than go down two or three times a day to check on her in her own house. Nigel was a babe in arms at the time and Heather had a lot on her hands. Her mother called for her from the bed she was in and it should be noted that there were no doors in our cottage. As Heather walked to the doorway, she could not go through as there seemed to be some sort of barrier. Heather realised what it was and called on Satan to leave our house and never to come back. She was immediately able to walk through the doorway and the first words she said to her mother was "Don't you ever bring Satan back into this house." There was another time when we visited her, it was around early morning and across her manicured lawn was the track of a single wheel mark. Heather's mum claimed that her husband had been there and pushed the wheelbarrow across the lawn. We told her it was most likely an evil spirit who had visited. Another occasion where we had issues with her was when she lived in our farm in the early eighties. She had given Heather several items and had done other jobs on the farm. She said back then that the items were either a birthday or a Christmas gift, depending on when it was given. She then decided that she should get paid for them all and sent us an account for just over $11,000 and demanded payment straightaway. We did pay her and told her not to bother coming back to the farm without our invitation, which has always been extended to her. She told us that she had cursed the farm and it would never do any good. I advised her that God is more powerful than her demons and that the farm would prosper. It did. After this, there was one day when sent me an African voodoo doll full of pins. She did occasionally visit the farm but only came as far as the front gate. She would hang a present on the gate for Heather, never for me. Mostly it was something she had cooked. I was always wary of these gifts and would always feed some to the dog, and if she was still well 48 hours later we decided that it must not be poisoned. I would always write and thank her for the gift. We get on okay now because she realises that we are the only sensible close relatives she has. But it is still a task to remain civil when we visit her. She has planned to be buried in an above-ground crypt in the Nudgee cemetery.

When I was courting Heather, it took several months before her mother worked out that I was visiting Heather and not her. She would ask me to visit her when she was ill (which was often) as she thought I had some kind of healing in my hands. It was a bit scary for me as a 16 year old to be asked to massage the breasts of my girlfriend's mother. I actually never went that far but I suppose I did give her some comfort, plus it also allowed me to be closer to where Heather was. This lady had several "boyfriends" while she was still married to Heather's dad. It was sad for him because he was such a gentleman. He was killed in a train crash at Narangba station on June 8 1970. He died of a literal broken heart. His heart was ruptured by the impact of the crash. There is much more could be written about this lady but suffice it to say that she was very different from most people.

ACCIDENT AT KANGAROO POINT

One morning, I was transporting a patient to Greenslopes hospital and I was in the middle of three lanes in heavy traffic just off the end of the Story Bridge. A Morris Z Ute was on my left, when suddenly the driver decided that he had to turn right in the next street about 60 yards ahead. He just turned left and hit me, taking out my front headlight and ripping the ambulance open right through to the taillight. My patient was thrown off the stretcher but thankfully he was not injured in the accident. After parking off the road, I went back to check if anyone had been injured in the prang. No one had been hurt. The driver of the Ute was getting around on crutches, and he only had one leg. He had one thought on his mind and that was to get the headlight from his car which was in the middle of a very busy road with a lot of traffic. He wanted me to get it for him, but I had a patient to look after and advised him if he really wanted it he would have to get it himself. Another ambulance arrived and took my patient off to the hospital. It is always risky driving in heavy traffic, you can always be doing the right thing and then along comes someone who does not conform.

LOST TELEPHONES.

Sometimes work would be very hectic and we would often spend days in a daze as the work continued. I have worked very long hours many, many times and it would take its toll on the body. Once at Caboolture I was on night duty and the phone rang. I was woken up and could not for the life of me find the phone, I was opening doors and cupboards all to no avail, and eventually the boss answered it. At another time out west, I was woken up at about midnight and I could not find the phone. Heather got up and found me in the wardrobe and asked me what I was doing, then she took me to the phone. Yes, the job of a paramedic was and can still be a very tiring career but nevertheless it is always rewarding. I was always able to get back to sleep after doing a job. Over the years, I trained myself to catch a nap whenever I could, sometimes even behind the wheel. I could sleep through any noise except for the ringing of a phone. I was able to sit in the lounge with a teaspoon in my hand and a metal plate on the floor, under the spoon. As soon as I dropped off to sleep the spoon would drop, hit the plate and I was instantly wide awake. To me this was equivalent to 5 hours of sleep. This is now called a NANA nap. I started doing this in the early 1970's. I am still able to nod off in a few minutes wherever I am.

Victor Torrens

SNIFFING PETROL FUMES

One time on a day off, I was driving near the weighbridge at Burpengary, with my family in the car. We began following this vehicle which was all over the road. I considered it too dangerous so I passed him and forced him to stop at the weighbridge. The driver immediately got out of his car and took off across the road and over to a house about half a mile away. The police were called and they rounded up the driver who was breathe tested and was found to be over the limit. He told the police that he had been shook up by being forced off the road and that he had gone to his mate's place and had a couple of stiff rums. There were other witnesses other than me, though. The case ended up in court. I was called as witness and one of the first questions I was asked was whether or not I drink. My response was, "Yes your honour, water." The driver's solicitor tried to have the case thrown out because he claimed that his client had been working on his car's engine and had his head under the bonnet for a long time and was affected by the fumes of the engine. Fortunately, this ruse did not work. The driver was found guilty and he spent time in jail. This solicitor was also a bit odd. One time, I treated him for an accident he had with a chainsaw. He had severely ripped his arm and almost severed one finger on his left hand. I told him I could dress it for him but he would have to go to the hospital for further treatment. I duly bandaged the injuries and off he went. Some weeks later I ran into him down the street and asked how his injuries were going. He said they were real good and showed me the scars. I asked him how many stitches he had received and he said none, because he did not go to the hospital, and that he just left the bandages I put in place for 10 days and he told me that as I can see it has healed up well, and it had. I guess he can be thankful that I was able to do a good job patching him up.

LITTLE BOY DROWNED

A call came in that a young lad was missing in Bellmere creek just near where it joined the Caboolture River. He had been swimming with some mates at the weir when he was washed away. The creek was in flood at the time. The lad was about nine.

After contacting the police and other rescue services, a search was conducted. The search area was about five miles of the creek and Caboolture River. I was given the task of telling the boy's parents that their son was missing and was most likely drowned. This was one of the hardest tasks I have ever had to do, especially since I knew the parents. It always broke my heart to some degree when I had to deliver these messages. We eventually found his body about three miles down the river under almost 12 feet of water.

WAR VETERANS

I have a couple of funny stories about World War I veterans who were in their 80s and 90s. One chap was called Riverman Mackie, he was named after I think 6 of Australia's best known rivers. He was a funny fellow in that he was always confused about most things. I would pick him up to go to Greenslopes hospital for treatment every two weeks. He would be good on the way to the hospital, but on our return trip he would start to make arrangements so he could sneak home, so that the Matron would not see him. He reckons she would scold him if he was late. When we got home near the War Vets home in Caboolture, he would direct us to a hole in the hedge. He reckons he could sneak in and not be seen. We would have to convince him that this was the best hole to go through.

Another chap would be picked up also every two weeks but on a different day. He was always dressed in a complete suit with a vest and a tie. As soon as he was in the ambulance he would ask if it was alright to have a smoke. My response was always "Okay." So he would put his hand into the inside pocket of his coat and pull out an imaginary packet of tobacco. First, he would take out a paper and stick it to his lip, then shake some tobacco onto one hand and commence to rub it into shape, then he would take the paper and roll a cigarette. Then there would be a problem, because you see, he never ever had any matches, so he would ask if I had a lighter. I would tell him where it was and he would get it and proceed to light the imaginary cigarette. Then he would need the ash tray opened and this series of comical events would happen all the way to the hospital and back.

Another man used to ask if it was alright to smoke while going to the hospital. "Yep it would be okay," I would tell him. He would then get a box of matches out, put one in his mouth, and endeavour to light it. I never once saw him get burnt as the matches would flare and then go out. He would continue to "smoke" the dead match all the way there and back. These men were real gentlemen and were always very polite, but we did get some laughs at their expense.

WHEN NATURE CALLED AT THE WRONG TIME

I answered the phone one morning at about 9am and I was told that a young man had been hit by a falling tree. In my experience, a falling tree does not bring about a good result. I responded and met the caller at a predetermined spot. I then followed a bulldozer as they made a road for me to drive on as the country was very steep and rough. After about three quarters of a mile we arrived at another bulldozer and the patient. It seems that they were scrub clearing with a massive chain about half a mile long, between two bulldozers. The young fellow, who was in his thirties, felt the call of nature and stopped for a leak. He stood on the track of the dozer, but did not tell the other dozer which kept going. As a result, the chain kept going and shook a large dead tree, which dropped a limb. This limb fell directly onto the fellow having a leak. It hit him on the right side of his body and damaged everything on the way down. Head, shoulder, ribs, pelvis, hip, and leg. He was in a real bad way. I did some preliminary treatment and I reckoned that if I did not get him to a doctor ASAP, he would surely die. I raced to get him to a private doctor in Caboolture who set up a couple of drips. Then, under police escort, I raced to get him to RBH where a team of doctors worked on him for about 2 hours. I assisted and my job was to manually pump the infusion kit to pour fluid into the man's body. Unfortunately, he did not survive, but we tried. He was married and had a couple of small children.

SNAKE BITE AND WIRE

One morning, a couple of old chaps living at Beachmere outside Caboolture were bushwalking and ran across a brown snake which promptly bit one of them on the ankle. This was a time before the "Snakebite Bandage" was known by the general public.

These fellows knew about tourniquets as a treatment for snakebites, so they talked about what to use for a tourniquet. Nothing could be found nearby except for some fencing wire. *Aha*, that will do. So a length was cut, doubled, and made into a Cobb & Co hitch. This was twitched up nice and tight with a short length of a broom handle. And then they phoned for help. I arrived about 10 minutes later and found the leg going blue. Believe me, the tourniquet was tight. It took me another few minutes to gradually release the wire and replace it with a bandage. I transported the patient to Redcliffe hospital for treatment, where he stayed for several weeks, not because of the snakebite but due to the damage done by the tourniquet.

ON THE MOVE

In 1973, we moved west for the health of our youngest son, Nigel. He was born with pyloric stenosis and it was a bad case. When he was three months old, he deteriorated overnight and went below his birth weight. He ended up in the Montrose home for incurably sick children. We went away for a few days as he would be having extensive tests and was not likely to survive for more than a few days at most. With my wife and two other children, we went for a tour around the Granite belt and Northern Rivers of NSW. My sister Lillian and her family also went with us. When we got back, Nigel had not only survived, the doctors had isolated the cause of his problem, and we were able to take him home, but we were advised that it would help him if we moved to a drier climate. I then applied for and got a job as a paramedic at Cloncurry. The next few stories are from that place.

We arrived at Cloncurry in June 1973 after an eventful trip out by the road. We commenced our trip with a 3-ton truck, our 1965 falcon wagon, and a trailer which my brother-in-law and I built in one night (it is now 2014 and I am still using the trailer). We left Caboolture at about 9am one weekday morning and we headed off on the Bruce Highway. We did not even get to Gympie before disaster struck.

I was driving our falcon wagon with a small caravan, and as I drove across Jackass Creek, where there was some roadwork going on, a semi came the other way. The mirror on the right side of his truck hit the caravan and opened it up from front to back. What a mess. There was stuff thrown out of the van everywhere. By the time I pulled up, Heather had arrived and she was sick when she realised that the stuff all over the bridge was ours. What should we do? We could not get the van fixed quickly and certainly not in Gympie. The accident happened about 7 kilometres south of Gympie. So we had to pack what we could into the car and the small truck we had and make our way to Maryborough where we managed to obtain another caravan and we left the damaged one there to be repaired under insurance.

We headed further north and arrived at Rockhampton. We stayed where we could each night, either beside the road or in a caravan park. After leaving Rockhampton, we decided that we would meet at the rest area near Marlborough for lunch. On the way there, there were some roadworks and our two vehicles got separated. Heather and my brother Phillip took a side track and ended up going through several properties and bush tracks. I arrived with the kids at Marlborough and after an hour or so I was getting concerned. Then suddenly, Heather and Phillip drove down a dirt road straight into the park from a totally different direction. I am sure the Lord directed their path that day as they drove almost twice the distance I did and still arrived at the same destination.

The trip to Cloncurry was interesting. Somewhere between Richmond and Julia Creek, the axle on the trailer snapped in half. Repairs were carried out with a length of 8 gauge fencing wire we "borrowed" from a nearby fence. This repair lasted until we got to Cloncurry where we were able to fit a new axle. This was the first time we had ever travelled so far out west and we were amazed at the vast distances, and at the same time we did get to love the country and the people.

Victor Torrens

YOU JUST CANNOT WORK WITH SOME PEOPLE

Cloncurry was a good place to work at. There was a large population of Aborigines in the town and at various settlements in the surrounding areas. As a family, we got on well with all the locals and enjoyed a good twelve months there until there was a change of superintendent at the ambulance. Working with Col Wheat was good and things changed when Col moved to Cairns. The new superintendent was Ted Pitman, a city person who was at best obnoxious to me and my family, as well as to the other people in town. I was not able to satisfy his work hour requirements. I was and still am a Seventh-day Adventist Christian, something that Ted would never accept. I would always ensure that the vehicles were clean and fuelled on Friday afternoon, even on my days off so that I would not have extra work to do on my Sabbath. I was always prepared to work on Sabbath but would only do what was necessary to ensure patients were looked after and treated right. On a few occasions, I would prepare the vehicles on Friday and turn up for work on Sabbath morning only to be told by Ted that I had better clean the cars. You see, he would scatter dirt and other stuff around the clean cars on Friday night to make sure I would have to do extra work on Sabbath. I was prepared to clean up after a patient had been sick or a car had got dirty from patients, but I strongly objected after the actions of Ted reached the third event. I refused to clean up and he told me that I had to do it or be sacked. I told him he made the mess, and he was not a patient, and therefore he could clean it up.

This was a situation which developed very quickly after Ted was appointed as superintendent. He treated me badly and also gave my wife and children a hard time, even before he had been there a month. One time I was held up at home with a water leakage problem and Ted stood at the back of the centre and whistled to me and yelled at me to come to work.

I advised him that I was not a dog and that he should rethink his attitude.

TRICKS THAT WORK

Sometimes I had to think smarter than my patients, the following stories are examples of this.

BLACK MAGIC

One night, I spent all night out on the road in a massive storm that covered the area from near Julia Creek out to Camooweal. It was raining considerably and there was constant lightning and thunder. At one point, Heather was looking after the station and anyone who came in. One aboriginal man called at about midnight and complained of a sore stomach. He was told to go home and to stop drinking metho, but he called in twice more before I got back. At about 2am, he called in again and still complained about having a sore stomach (this is what metho drinking will do to you). I told him I could do nothing for him and away he went again, only to come back in half an hour. By this time, I was wondering what I could do to get him out of my hair for the rest of the night. Sure enough, he was back again in a short while, but this time I was ready with some magic treatment for him. We were using at that time some Borofax cream for bites and stings. It was snow white and good for its purpose. When He returned yet again, I asked him to take his shirt off and promptly squirted almost a whole tube of Borofax onto his belly. Now this would never actually help his situation, but it worked psychologically on him. I rubbed it in and made his belly white. I asked him if it had helped and sure enough, it had. He marched off down the street with his shirt still off and he explained to his drunken mates how good it felt to not have a sore belly anymore.

MORE BLACK MAGIC

Another time, I was at the Burketown races for the weekend on a late Saturday evening and I was busy with drunks and the results of brawls. One big strapping young Aboriginal came to me with tears in his eyes as he was complaining of a sore wrist. I examined it for him and I could see no obvious injury. I sent him on his way after finding out what had happened. The story went like this: he was involved in a brawl over a bottle of "plonk" and when his mate hit him on the wrist with it, the bottle broke and the contents spilt onto the ground. I think this was the reason for the tears. Anyhow, sometime later he was back still complaining about a sore wrist, and still drunk as ever. What should I do? *Aha*, an idea. We used Elastoplast for strapping joint injuries on footballers. Perhaps, just perhaps, it might work. So I went out with a full roll and commenced to roll his wrist with the sticky stuff. Again, I had a psychological win and he went away happy and I did not see him again. I am not sure if he took it off or left it there for weeks until it fell off, but I do know it would never have helped his injury improve.

I also got called up to a patient near the Cloncurry airport who apparently was involved in some sort of Aboriginal payback attack. This was just after dark and the patient was in a bad way. We had no idea how long he had been laying in the bush, but blood was congealed all over him. I'm not sure why he was attacked or by whom, it's not really my concern, but whoever it was did a good job. The only bone in his body that was not broken was his pelvis. I treated him and off to hospital we went. He was later transferred to Townsville for further treatment. I never heard what he was beaten for. The police never got involved and to my knowledge no one was ever charged for the assault. He did eventually get over the attack and came back to town.

DRUGS IN SPORT

Sometimes a football coach would ask me for advice on how to pep up their players who may have been a bit hung over from a heavy night before the game. I had concocted a brew for them to drink. This was a mixture of ammonia and smelling salts diluted at about 1 tablespoon per litre of water, and a small glass was given to the players to drink just before the game started. It seemed to have a great effect on their stamina and also after some trials we found that it would allow them to run at a greater speed than normal. One young fellow who was very quick and could cover 100 yards in 12 seconds would regularly cut 1- 1½ seconds of a hundred-yard dash. I will not claim to have been the first person who used drugs to enhance player ability, but I may well have been, as this was back in 1973 when I started using this brew.

THE CALL OF NATURE AND TRAINS

One night at about 9pm, a call came in that a person had fallen from a train and could not be found, as no one knew where they were when he fell off the train. It appeared that a flying gang (Railway repair gang) were moving from Richmond to Cloncurry and one of the men, a large South Sea Islander, stood in the doorway to urinate and just as he did so the carriage jinked on a crossing and he fell out. They could not do anything about it until they got to Cloncurry station. We were called out as part of a search party and there were people looking up and down the line for miles. I was on a flat top wagon behind a motorised trolley with lights and torches looking as we went. After about two hours, we still had no sign of the fellow. So we went over the same country again and this time we did find someone sitting beside a mileage peg about 30 kilometres from Cloncurry. He was dazed but otherwise unhurt. It seemed that when he fell out of the train, he hit this mileage peg and he was knocked out. We only found him after he became conscious again. His being black made it much harder for us to find him.

Now, you will not believe what happened next. At about 2am, we received a call from the railway advising us that another person had fallen from a train. This time it was in a very inaccessible part of the line between Cloncurry and Duchess on the Mount Isa line. This happened when an old Aboriginal had a fight with his wife and he got real angry and jumped from the train. We had just started the search when we got another message to say that the wife had also jumped, because she believed her husband would be dead and she might as well be also. This rescue ended with both people being uninjured and rescued safe and sound. Both were sober by this time.

BLACK SOIL AND FLAT TYRES

I received a call one night to attend to an incident out near Corindi, east of Cloncurry. From what I remember, it was a male patient from a drilling rig who had been injured and needed hospital treatment. To get to the site, I had about 40 kilometres of bitumen road and about 20 kilometres of dirt, and as I was driving out it started to rain and it steadily got heavier. I was able to get out to the rig, then I treated and loaded the patient and started back home and by this time the rain had just about stopped. If you have ever driven on outback roads, you will know what happened next. Because the rain had stopped, the black soil started to set like clay. It is okay while it is raining, but as soon as it stops, the soil will clog up under your car. This is what happened before I got back to the bitumen. The only way to fix it is to have a small crow bar and literally prise the mud from around the wheel and wheel well, as it jams the tyres and they will not even turn around. I cleaned the tyres a couple of times and then I noticed that I had a flat tyre. I was not about to change the tyre on the dirt section so I drove with the flat until I reached the bitumen. It was still a very muddy job to change it but at least I was laying on bitumen to get the spare off and not in the mud. I eventually got my patient to the hospital for treatment.

PLANES AND SICK ABORIGINES

This next story transpired over one whole night, one of the worst nights in my career. It happened during the 1974 flood which devastated a large amount of country and people in the west, even though reports suggest that Brisbane was the only area really damaged at this time. I received a call telling us that a small plane was desperately trying to find a landing strip in this massive storm which covered an area from Boulia to Camooweal, Richmond to west of Mount Isa. We heard the plane several times but we never saw it. We heard early next morning that seven young Adventist people from Avondale College on a mission trip to Darwin were all killed together with the pilot when the plane was apparently hit with lightning when it tried to land on a bush strip at the

Barkly Downs station. We knew one of the young people in that plane.

Now, back to the story. I got a call to an Aboriginal settlement out past Quamby, north of Cloncurry. The patient had a stroke and was really unwell. I headed off in the rain and for miles I went through water 12 to 15 inches deep, which was okay as I was driving a 4X4. I got to Quamby and the patient was brought in on a railway quad. After some treatment he was loaded and off we went to hospital. We did not get far as we drove through water until we got to a flooded creek and four feet of water over the road. What should I do next? I contacted the railway and I was told that there was an engine in Quamby that may be able to help and also a guards van. We accepted this offer but did not know how we would be able to utilise it. The railway line was about three quarters of a mile from the road where we were and we were unable to return to Quamby as the water had risen behind us. We waited for the train to arrive in the distance and then decided that the only way we could get the patient from the ambulance to the train was to carry him through three quarters of a mile of chest deep water with much grass and shrubs that would impede our progress. The patient weighed about 120 kilograms (20 stone) and was totally incapacitated. So, six of us loaded the stretcher with the patient onto our shoulders and off we set. What a journey it was as we struggled all the way until eventually getting to the train. With the patient safely on board we started towards Cloncurry and went well for several miles until we came across a bridge which had been damaged by floodwater. The driver was prepared to try and get across as our patient was going downhill fast. There were several sleepers that had been washed away from the bridge supports, so with me offering a silent prayer for safety, the driver very gently got the train across the bridge and we finished our trip to Cloncurry where we had another ambulance waiting for us to take the patient to the hospital. The patient unfortunately died early the next day.

BIG FLOODS

During our time in Cloncurry at around '73 to '74, we were out there during the great flood. This was a time of great distress for many people, as food became very scarce and people were unable to go anywhere. In those days, air travel was limited. We were fortunate that the day before the whole rail line from Mount Isa to Townsville was washed out we had received a good food order from Grantham. This order consisted of a sack of potatoes, onions, carrots, and several boxes of fruit. We always had a good supply of tinned food in the cupboard. It took many months before regular supplies started to come out our way. We never told anyone about our supply, as people were desperate and hungry. We did help a lot of people during this time. There were about 40 travellers stranded on the Cloncurry train station, and as members of the Lions club out there, we took on the task of feeding them one meal per day. It was hard to get food for them. One time, a large cargo plane landed in Mount Isa with food for Woolworths and I was asked if I would go and get some food so we could keep feeding these people. Woolworths had promised the Lions club a supply. I hooked the trailer on and away we went, with the advice from the police to carry my gun and not to stop for anyone on the road. We also went shopping in Woolworths and got caught up in a riot, literally. People were queued up for about three miles along the streets and were only allowed to obtain a specified quantity of food per person. One woman who had a new baby was taking two large bottles of milk through the checkout, but the limit was one so she had to go to the back of the queue and start again. One of the staff members brought a pallet of potatoes out into the store, then people went mad scrambling to get their 1 kilo packet. The poor fellow had his arm broken in the riot. We got our food supplies and headed home. There was no problem with the trip and we were able to feed the people again. One grazier was stranded for weeks on the roof of his house during this flood and had to eat his blue heeler to keep alive. A lot of personal trauma was probably formed out there.

LITTLE GREEN MEN

I was called out one night to a sheep property out near Duchess, SW of Cloncurry. A shearer's cook was having problems. He had been drinking whatever he could get hold of. Quite a lot of these men were alcoholics and when beer was hard to get they would drink whatever. This chap had apparently been drinking strait lemon essence and strained boot polish, and he was in a bad way. After getting him settled in the front seat of the ambulance, we headed to town. We were almost there when he suddenly asked me to stop while we were at the western side of the Curry River. I thought nature was calling, but no, he dashed out of the car straight into the headlights and proceeded to tear his trousers off. At the same time, he was screaming and yelling about the "little green men." What should I do? I could not see anything but had to settle him down somehow.

I eventually talked him into getting dressed again and told him to get back into the car. He refused and told me, "I can't, there are green men on the seat." Bush psychology again to the fore, I chased the "green men" out of the car and he got in. We finished the trip only to confront more "little green men" on his bed at the hospital. The poor nurses could do nothing with him. I again chased them out of the room, to the astonishment of the nursing staff. They then had no more trouble with the patient.

SABBATH PROBLEMS

After about 8 months at Cloncurry, there was a change of superintendent. Col Wheat left for Cairns and Ted Pitman was appointed to Cloncurry. Ted was a new superintendent and knew little about staff management and had only ever worked in the city of Brisbane. He actually knew little about most things, and he was not prepared to learn. My appointment conditions allowed me to have my Sabbath duties restricted to emergencies. Other work, cleaning cars, and housework was either done on my previous day on or I would make sure all was in order even if the Friday was my day off. Poor Ted was not able to accept this and demanded that I do all cleaning and other duties on my Saturday roster. I declined his offer and things only got worse from that point. Ted would make sure that if I cleaned the station and cars on my Friday off, that there would be grass, dirt, and untidy beds in the cars and station when I came to work on Saturday. I felt that this was totally unfair and I kindly told him as much, but he refused to rethink his ideas. When I offered to explain to him my reasons for only doing emergencies on Sabbath, he refused to listen and stated that if I was prepared to work emergencies then I would have to attend to other duties as well. This situation could not continue, for me at least, so I started to apply for another position at Hughenden. This position had been open for 18 months with the proviso that it was only a six-month trial to see if the workload warranted another full time officer. When the job was recalled the next month, which was May, it was then for a full time position. I applied and was given the position.

During this time of trouble, Bob Katter Jnr, State Member for Cloncurry, had offered to get me a job as a counsellor at the Charters Towers Aged Care Home. I seriously thought about this, but my love for the paramedic life prevailed.

I promptly resigned from my position at Cloncurry, even though Ted had already stated that I was to be sacked. I just beat him to the punch that was how bright he was. He also stated that the fellow I was going to work for at Hughenden was no angel. My response was that the fellow I am now working for is no angel and I know that because I did know him, and I had as yet not met Ken Eagle, the superintendent at Hughenden who turned out to be quite a decent man to work for.

HUGHENDEN

I started at Hughenden in July 1974, after a brief holiday in Brisbane with my family.

Our time at Hughenden was enjoyable and is full of wonderful memories. We were there for just over 5 years and after many adventures, we left with a lot of stories to tell.

As soon as we arrived in Hughenden, we purchased a house, and we lived in that house until we moved to Thursday Island.

XU1 TORANA

One of the first accidents I attended to at Hughenden involved a young couple in a Torana XU1. At around 1am on a Sunday morning, they were driving at excessive speeds down a dirt road about 4 kilometres out of town. When I arrived, the car was a wreck. It apparently had rolled nose to tail 11 times after hitting a ditch that was 4 feet deep and about 12 feet wide. I only found one patient, the driver who was still in the car. He had terrible injuries and his head was literally turned back to front. What should I do? He was alive but only just. I had to treat the whole body, there were massive fractures and other soft tissue injuries. My first task was to attempt to re-align his head to the right position. With a prayer and some deft positioning, I was able to do this, although it did not improve his condition. I transported him to the hospital and after unloading him, I was told that his wife would have been with him. I had not seen her so I went back to the scene with some helpers and eventually located her about 60 feet from the first point of impact. She had been thrown out and was killed instantly. Her father arrived as I got back to the hospital with her body. He was in denial of the fact that she was dead. He was trained in CPR and he attempted to revive her. After half an hour, I was able, with police help, to convince him that she was deceased. What a dreadful time it was for him and for us. It is upsetting enough to have to deal with death, but grieving relatives can be harrowing.

The husband was stabilised, albeit in a complete coma, and arrangements were made to transport him to the Townsville hospital for specialist treatment. An Orion aircraft was flown out from the Army base at Townsville with several doctors on board to look after the patient on the trip to Townsville.

With much care and difficulty, the patient was placed into the aircraft and strapped down. I then saw some specialist equipment which I had never seen before. The neurosurgeon who was on board placed a whisp of cotton wool onto the patient's top lip with plaster. I was intrigued by this and I asked the reason for it. His response was that the aircraft is so noisy and the vibrations are so bad that they are unable to properly see if the patient is breathing so they would just watch the cotton wool and if it flutters then it would mean that the patient is still breathing. I think this was a means used during wartime evacuations.

This young man passed away about 48 hours later when his family made the decision to turn off his life support. His organs were used to save other very ill patients. This lad was a very good footballer and could run 100 meters in under 12 seconds, which he did regularly under the right conditions.

We had a lot of calls out to a well-known Aboriginal residential area and several times I was put at risk by someone who was drunk there. It was not always the same person but there were enough of them to make it scary at times. Our response to this was always to call and advise the police, who would come out as well.

IN A HEADLOCK

One incident involved a young Aboriginal woman, who had a badly cut wrist involving an artery, and she was losing a lot of blood. Back then at 1974, we did not know much about aids, so my first response was to grab her wrist and put pressure on to stop the bleeding. As I did so, one of the young bucks promptly grabbed me in a headlock and accused me of holding his girlfriend's hand. I promptly let go and just at this time the police arrived. He released my head and the police asked if they could help. I told them to put the man into the paddy wagon before his girlfriend passed out from loss of blood. After this I was able to treat her and safely take her to the hospital.

BE CAREFUL IF YOU FALL DOWN THE STEPS

Another incident involved a woman who was about 40 years old. I was called to attend to a woman who had supposedly fallen down some steps and injured herself. This time the police did not respond so I was there by myself. The woman had no clothes on and was literally skinned back and front. She was about 5 feet tall and was quite plump. She was in a mess, and was losing quite an amount of blood. The boyfriend was there who after being asked explained that this happened to her when she fell down the steps at the back of the house. I was amazed as the house was only one step off the ground. The boyfriend's mother and father were also there and they backed his story up. It took a while for me to treat this lady and get her to hospital, still shaking my head as to the amount of skin taken off this woman by falling down one step. Of course I could not believe their story, so the police were advised and they got the correct story. It seems as though the couple had a history of violence and after an argument he had literally grabbed the woman by the hair, which was quite long, and dragged her up and down a concrete slab about 30 feet long leading out to the clothes line at the back of the house. This continued until she had no clothes left on and hardly any skin left. The boyfriend spent some time at her majesty's pleasure for his efforts.

We spent our time off at Hughenden by looking at some of the country around about. It is a beautiful part of Queensland and is worth looking at. Below are some of the highlights from our 5 years there.

PORCUPINE GORGE

My sister Lillian and her husband Pat and their children were there for most of our time. Pat got some part-time work but was unemployed for the most part. Their youngest, Pamela, was born in Hughenden. For Christmas day in 1974, we decided to spend the day exploring Porcupine Gorge, which was about 60 or so kilometres north of Hughenden. What a great place it was, although at that time it was a very difficult climb in and out of the Gorge. Pat and I went fishing along the gorge without any fishing gear. The rest of the family was amazed when we turned up with about 20 or so good fish. They would not believe we had caught them, they reckoned there had to be someone else fishing there. It was true that we caught the fish. We did so by hand in a pool of water only about 2 feet deep along the creek. The fish were no good to eat though as they were bony bream. We had a lovely time down there and still talk about it today.

It was not until we got back to town that we heard about the terrible disaster that had befallen Darwin, "Cyclone Tracy." For several months after this event, we had people coming through Hughenden who had been through the cyclone, and you could see the result in their eyes and the way they talked about it reflects how it affected them all.

There were and still is a lot of fossils out in that country. We found dinosaur bones and fossilised fish in several locations around the area. It is well known that the area was at one time an inland sea.

LOSING YOUR SHOES

I saw the result of a fatal accident near Hughenden that I had only heard about and have never seen since. At about 8pm one night, I got called to an accident near Torrens Creek about 60 kilometres east of town. Upon arrival, I found a deceased male who was about 60 or so. He had been hit by a vehicle travelling at 100kph. The story was that a vehicle travelling east had hit a large pig and broken its back, and it was still on the road and the driver got out to try and slow down an oncoming car. Unfortunately, the first driver had left his car in the middle of the road and with the lights on high beam. This somewhat blinded the oncoming car and they did not see the driver standing in their lane. This driver said he thought it was a kangaroo and did not take much evasive action. When he hit the patient who was standing, the latter was blown out of his shoes which were still where he had been standing. His body was many meters away, and he was obviously killed on impact. I had heard about people being blown out of their shoes by violent impact but had never seen it before nor since.

TO WORK ON SABBATH OR NOT

At various times during my career I had to attend sporting functions on Sabbath, in case of emergencies. One time, I was at the races in Hughenden on Sabbath afternoon when we got a call about a person burnt in an explosion at Torrens Creek, east of Hughenden. The boss was away and I was working by myself. I arranged for the second ambulance to be brought out to the race track for the police to operate if needed. I proceeded to Torrens Creek. When I got there, I was advised that a man who was about 45 had been burnt quite badly by a petrol explosion. I treated him and headed back to the hospital. This patient was later transferred by plane to Brisbane for specialist burns treatment. Remember that this was the Sabbath.

On Monday, I received another call to go to Torrens Creek where a railway worker had broken his arm when an engine he was cranking backfired and kicked him. He was probably in his mid-twenties. I treated him and headed back to the hospital. On the way back, he started to complain about his mate who had been burnt on Saturday and had to wait several hours, until after sunset, to be treated because the ambulance officer was one of those weirdos who will not work on Saturday. He said his mate was in a bad way and there should be a law about people not working on so called "religious days." I let him get it off his chest and then advised him that I was the officer who picked up his friend on Saturday, and treated and transported him to hospital during daylight hours. He never apologised for not stating the truth, but he did keep quiet for the rest of the trip, which lasted about 45 minutes.

FIRST AID AND SNAKES

I had the opportunity to teach a first aid class somewhere north of Hughenden, though I can't remember the station name. I had the weekend off so I took my wife and three kids with me. The trip took an hour and a half and we arrived at about 8:30 and started the course at nine. We were only covering snake bites and CPR, which took us up till lunch time. There were about 16 or so property owners there who supplied us all with a lovely lunch. Afterwards, it was time for a look around. We were walking down from the house with our kids and their kids, a dozen or so of them running ahead of us. Suddenly someone yelled, "Snake!" and for the first time ever I saw a heap of kids just freeze. There was a massive king brown between two of the kids who were about 10 feet apart. The snake was reared up about two feet off the ground. One of the owners had a gun and managed to despatch the snake in no time. I am glad we did not have to practice what I had just taught. Our daughter Rose was one of the two kids. Both were about 10 at the time.

APPRECIATION OF CATTLE

One time during a day off, we went as a family for a drive north of Hughenden, just to enjoy the scenery. It was a dry time of the year. We came across a dam which was basically dry with just mud across an area of about 50 square feet in the middle. There was a cow stuck in the middle of the mud, buried to her waist. We had ropes so we decided it would be good if we got her out. Alan and Nigel who were eight and six at this time were ready for any adventure, so I made a noose with the rope and sent the boys in to hook it over her horns. They got down and dirty real quick and they got the rope on and with a lot of encouragement we managed to pull the cow out with the 4X4. The boys got the rope off, and then had to run like crazy because the cow chased them and then promptly went back into the bog. The second time was better as she stayed out.

TRAINS AND BEDROOMS

There was an old European fellow at Hughenden, a carpenter by trade who was known locally as "White ant" presumably because of his work. One morning at about 3am, we got a call to the railway yard, and upon arrival we find "White ant" hanging onto the cow catcher of the steam train and complaining loudly that the %#@&*@, train had driven straight through his bedroom. He was a bit of a mess but the situation was not life-threatening. He was of course dead drunk.

BOGGED IN BULLDUST

At Hughenden, I also started a system of collecting subscriptions and it worked well, and the centre became very financial. While collecting, I would stay at the property where I was at around 5pm for the night. I was always very well looked after, sometimes the owner would give me directions to a shortcut from their property to the next, which could save me up to an hour of driving. On one of these shortcuts, I rounded a bend (dirt track) and promptly fell into a huge patch of bulldust. Bogged to the axles in a falcon wagon. If you have ever tried digging bull dust out you will know it is like digging water with a shovel. After about 2 hours, I had managed to get enough grass and sticks under the wheels for traction and just managed to get out. I was also lucky to find a turkey's nest (waterhole) where I could have a wash and change before I reached the next property.

RODEOING

We were heavily involved with the Rodeo at Hughenden, I was in the Lions club as either Secretary or President at various times. The Lions club owned a string of about 150 brumbies used for the Rodeo. These horses were mustered the weekend before the Rodeo. They were taken to the cattleyards, sorted out and then taken to the showground via the main street of town. It was always exciting for everyone to see 100-plus wild horses surging at full gallop through town.

Len and Margaret Hoare became very good friends of ours while we were at Hughenden. They owned the soft drink factory. We're still great friends they're now living near Mackay.

FRIENDS AND HORSES

Another family we became good friends with is the Pearce family who lived at Torrens Creek. Albert and Daphne had six or seven children and had a cattle property. We often went and helped them with farm work such as mustering and the like. Albert had some real crazy horses which were always hard to ride and manage as they were mostly retired or useless race horses. One would always throw you at some time throughout the day. I remember once riding helter skelter after a runaway beast and the horse was hard to control. It used to throw its head sideways and you never knew which side of an obstacle it was going to run. We came to a tree which the beast had just passed and of course the horse did not know which side to go. I then went on one side and the horse went the other. Help would always come once the horse got home and we'd have another story to tell and laugh about.

BEWARE THE GRASSHOPPERS

I was due to start my annual leave on Saturday morning when at about 10:30pm I received a call to a fitting patient who was about an hour and a half drive away to the north of Hughenden. I was almost there when I hit a kangaroo which damaged the front panels of my vehicle and also busted the fanbelt. I managed to drive slowly to the property afterwards. The patient had ceased fitting once I arrived, so it was time for a cuppa. It was about 1am. While we were having a drink, the station owner found a fan belt and fitted it for me. I eventually loaded the patient onto the stretcher and started back towards home. We travelled for about an hour with no problems with the patient but we hit another kangaroo. Not much damage was done to the car but the patient began fitting again. By the time we got to the hospital the patient was in a grand fit. I guess it's time for our holiday now. We drove to Brisbane.

I arrived back at work on a Sunday six weeks later, and I started work on Sunday evening. At about 9pm, I got a call to transfer a young patient from Hughenden to Townsville. The patient was injured from a horse accident. Arrangements were made to meet a Charters Towers Ambulance half way, near Pentland. It was a good trip so far until I was about 5 kilometres through Pentland when another kangaroo had me in its sights. This time real damage was done, and I had to stop. Fortunately, the Towers vehicle arrived within a few minutes. We transferred the patient and the police arranged for me to spend the night in jail. (This was the only bed available in town as there was a Rodeo on and all other accommodations were taken.)

TENNIS ANYONE

As a young man, I was an average to reasonably good tennis player and I played for many years growing up. I was able to win a few trophies when I played. While at Hughenden, we would often use the tennis courts at the hospital to play. One time there was a South African Doctor there and we invited him to join us. Before coming to Australia, he was the personal dentist of Idi Amen, the dictator. This lovely doctor advised us that he knew nothing about the game called tennis so we had to explain to him how it was played. We decided to just practice hitting the ball over the net at first. Eventually, it was time to have a proper game. Well, did we learn a lesson? It turns out he was a champion tennis player and he wiped us off the court. You just never can tell sometimes.

BUTCHER SHOP

I had a story related to me from the police regarding a couple of Aboriginal lads who wanted to butcher a steer they had, though I do not know if it was theirs or not. Anyhow, the story goes that these two energetic lads eventually got the beast up the steps and into the lounge of their rented house, where they promptly cut its throat and started to butcher it. All was going well until the sun went down and they found themselves in the dark. You see, the lounge had a blown light bulb. Not to be stopped, these two enterprising lads quickly worked out that the bulb in the adjoining room worked perfectly well, but they were not electricians so they were not about to change bulbs. So they promptly took to the partition with a chain saw and cut a big hole in the wall. Problem solved, they could now see to continue their task. They received a holiday in the big house for their trouble.

I'M NOT SCARED

I went for a 4x4 drive up the Flinders River sometime in 1978. The river was dry and full of sand as it always was. We loaded our kids and our gear in our Land Cruiser. My brother-in-law Pat packed his wife and kids into their little Second World War jeep and off we went. We had a safe drive up and down the river, and eventually found a good spot for a campfire and bar-b-que tea. After we ate, we spent some time around the campfire to tell stories. Pat snuck off into the long grass and after a while he made some grunting noises. The kids all heard this and decided it was a wild pig. So off they went to investigate. Stephen, Pat & Lil's son, was the oldest and biggest of all the five kids so he led the way. Stephen grabbed a large lump of wood from near the fire with which to fight off the "pig." All the other kids were following along behind Stephen when suddenly the "pig" let out with a tremendous roar. Stephen dropped the piece of wood as he turned and bolted, flattening all the other kids in his path. He told us that he was not scared and it was just the noise that frightened him. The other kids were spread out all over the area.

THURSDAY ISLAND

Towards the end of 1979, I applied for and was appointed as superintendent at Thursday Island. We had to pack up and have our furniture transported to T.I. via boat. We contacted a removal truck and when they arrived in town, the first four people the driver asked about our address told him that they did not know where we lived. I found out later that the townsfolk did not want us to leave. I guess we did not want to leave either but the position was a promotion and it presented a great adventure.

I started work on Thursday Island on December 11, 1979, and what a different place to work it was. I asked our Islander friend who lived in Hughenden to come with us and show us around but he told me, "No way Vic, they are too black for me." He also gave me good advice on how to get things done on the Island.

I THINK MY WIFE IS PREGNANT

We were only on the Island for five days when I received a phone call from an Islander. We used to struggle to understand them on the phone, which was connected through an exchange. The Islanders would talk to you through the glass door of the phone box into the mouthpiece, and generally had very muffled voices.

This particular call was from a male who advised me that he thought his wife was pregnant and asked if I could come and check her out. Well, with a request like that how could I refuse! Heather asked me what I would do when I got there. I replied that I would have a look and see if she was pregnant. Would you believe it? She was. I delivered a very healthy baby boy, the first I had actually delivered by myself. The next day, which was a Saturday, I received a call from a lady Islander. She introduced herself as the woman who got hot water, towels, and other stuff for me at the delivery. I asked how I could help and she wanted to know if they could name the baby after me. It took some time and a lot of questions to establish my family history and the baby was named Victor Torrens Gibuma. For three weeks after that I would check the front porch each morning until Heather asked me what I was looking for at the front door. I told her that they will leave that baby there for us to have. This did not happen though. We have heard that this lad is all grown up and has accepted the Seventh-day Adventist religion, which is what our faith is. One day we may get the opportunity to find him.

TRAFFIC POLICE

I got called out one night at about 1am to a girl who had been attacked. On T.I., there was probably about 100 vehicles all up, so as I drove around to the address to have a look at this patient, I came to a crossroads in a suburb in Tamwoy town. Lo and behold, there was a traffic cop directing traffic. He was one of T.I.'s native policemen. He waved me through although at that time of night I think I was the only vehicle moving on the Island. I then arrived at what I thought was the house where the patient was. You need to know that street numbers on T.I., when they were visible, were different. The numbers went 1-9 down one side of the street and 10-20 down the other. I knocked on the door and got no answer so I decided to go next door when I promptly ran into a massive Islander with no clothes. This is enough to get the brain wondering. After wishing the naked man a good evening I knocked on the next house, and was told to come around the back. Intrigued, I did so. I knocked on the back door and a voice asked who it was and I identified myself as the ambulance man. With that, the door was opened and a black arm shot out, grabbed me, and dragged me inside. I found myself in a house full of women, some of which were crying. I asked what the matter was and was told that a young girl had been attacked. She was okay as the attacker never got to do what he intended, thankfully. I did not take her to the hospital but after giving some advice and calming everyone down, I headed home. I pulled up at the T.I. Police barracks on the way and I reported the attack and the meeting with the naked man. The response I got was, "Oh, he is at it again is he, we will pick him up tomorrow and have a talk with him." They were obviously very involved in the card game that was going on.

STIFF AS A BOARD

We had a patient on T.I. who we would pick up quite regularly. He loved his drink and was often drunk. He also loved to eat and drink whatever else he could get hold of that might give him a high. One day he mixed up a concoction which contained quite a bit of glue hardener which rendered him unconscious. When I took him to the hospital, the doctor was concerned that he might die, but I was advised by the nursing staff that he would be okay and that if he did die, he would at least be "stiff as a board."

CROCODILES AND BABIES

I received a call one night from a Catholic priest, who was one of our honorary officers, informing me of a young girl who was having a baby. She was in labour and on Hammond Island. Arrangements were made for a dinghy to go and pick her up, with me and three Islanders to carry the gear and the stretcher. This was at about 1am. So off into the night we went. We went about 3 kilometres across the channel behind T.I and through about 2 kilometres of mangrove swamp to the village. We picked up the girl and made our way back to the hospital. The doctor said he was going home to bed and he left me to assist with the birth. About two hours later, I delivered a healthy baby girl by myself in the theatre. It was a rewarding experience. Later that day, I was talking to the priest who advised me that the mangrove swamp is known as a haunt for several crocodiles. I'm glad I did not know that beforehand, or else the girl may have had the baby at home.

At one point, I was able to travel by helicopter on the mail run out to several islands. It was a lovely trip. On the way back, we were travelling along the western end of T.I when the chopper suddenly went into a slide and turned around. When I asked the pilot what was happening he said, "Look down at the water's edge," and there was a massive crocodile which the pilot said was probably 16-18 feet long. He reported it because it was only about 100 or so yards from the Japanese pearling station. We thought that it may have been waiting for a Japanese take away meal.

FISHING

Alan and Nigel spent a lot of time fishing off the wharf using prawn heads they got from the prawn factory as bait. Most days, they would catch a decent feed and they'd be followed home by the little island kids, who would sometimes say, "Look at him catch big fish."

One time I got a call to attend to an accident on a fishing boat, a female deck hand had fallen into the winch compartment and got her leg caught on the pulleys. Her ankle was injured as the pulley had been spinning on it. We gave her treatment and then got her off the boat and up to the hospital. As I left the boat, the skipper told me to come back once we finish at the hospital and he will give me a feed of fish. Food being at a premium, I took him up on the offer. I went back to the boat and he gave me a massive 7-foot-long king salmon. I wrapped it in a sheet and placed it on the stretcher. When I got back to the station I had to borrow an electric saw from the builder next door to cut the fish up into 2-inch thick steaks. It was a beautiful fish that lasted for weeks.

FIRST AID

I was able to teach several first aid courses while on Thursday Island. It was great to teach kids but I also learned much from them. It took me three weeks to get the kids confident enough to know that the ambulance phone number was number 1. There was always trouble when it came to teaching CPR though. The boys and girls would balk at doing chest compressions on the mannequin. They would turn away and say, (sou-sou) breasts. But eventually I was able to convince them that there was nothing wrong about touching the dummy, and that they would do okay with the sessions. Answering questions was another matter. I remember once, the paper had a question: "What would you do with someone who had a broken leg?" One student answered that he would place him on his head, in the corner with all the other broken legs. At least triage would be solved. Peter Holt, the surgeon at the hospital, and I had many a laugh over the answers. After the course was finished, the students would invite my wife, me and the family to a special meal prepared by them. It was always a good evening.

LOST ON A BIKE RIDE

One early morning at around 3am, I had taken a patient who needed a doctor to the hospital. The doctor lived in a set of units in town about two kilometres from the hospital and would often ride a pushbike when called in. We called but 45 minutes went by and we received no response. We thought that the doctor had gone back to sleep but we called him again. We were told that he had already left so we waited a while longer. He eventually turned up with his pushbike on his shoulder. He explained that he was riding through an old quarry on the main road when all of a sudden he ran into a mob of Islanders who were camped on the road while having a drinking session. No one was injured but the bike was a mess.

HOW TO SPEND YOUR HARD-EARNED MONEY

Several Islanders worked as pearl divers for the pearl factory and they would get fairly good money, but the work was hard and dangerous as they would often go down up to 60 feet deep to get a pearl shell without any breathing gear. One time, a diver came home after working for about a month without any time off and he had a pocket full of money. To stop his mates and family from bumming all his money, he hired one of the few taxis on the island and spent almost a week with four of his mates just driving around the island until he had drank away all his money. He then packed up and went back to diving. I guess it was a break.

COPYCATS

The Islanders were pretty good copycats as we were able to find out. We bought each of our kids a kite and once they had them flying, within a few days there were kites all over the island, tangled in trees, power lines and rooftops. It was quite funny. Another time, the kids wanted to feel a bit safer on the beach so we spent some time picking up broken bottles and other rubbish. Very soon, there were whole Islander families also picking up rubbish along the beaches.

GUNFIGHT

I was woken up early one morning to the sound of gunshots. This went on for about 15 minutes with everyone wondering what was happening. It appears that a couple of Islanders got hold of some guns and decided to have some shooting practice along the beach. Very soon the police arrived and more shots were fired. A couple of arrests were made but fortunately no one was injured.

CHOOSE YOUR WEAPONS

One never knows how people are going to be injured in a domestic dispute. I got called to a house once, and I could tell by the noise on the phone that a domestic dispute was happening. I drove to the house and I was met by an island man with blood streaming from a wound on his head. I patched him up and on the way to the hospital I asked him what happened. He told me that he and his wife were having an argument when she whacked him on the head. I asked if she used a saucepan, but no, he said, she used a can of baked beans.

I also received a call to attend to a brawl at one of the local pubs. Upon arrival, I was escorted into the lounge area where around 8-10 women were having a dispute while playing billiards. One of them came over to me while she had blood pouring out of her head, I was endeavouring to find the damage when next thing I knew a billiard cue landed on her head. I thought to myself, "Vic, what are you doing here?" It was dangerous so I picked up my first aid kit, moved into a corner, sat down, and watched them fight for about another 10 or so minutes. Afterwards, I was able to treat all the injuries which were fortunately superficial and I transported six of them in one ambulance to the hospital for sutures.

PICNIC TIME

Work was very busy and demanding all the time when we were on T.I., but our family did manage to get one day off in 12 months. This was a great experience as the Lions club (I was a member) had an annual picnic over on Prince of Wales Island. We travelled as a family on the charter boat and landed on a lovely beach. It was a great day with fun and games for the kids and the adults had a great chance to talk and collect new memories.

PRACTICING WITCH DOCTORS

There were several well-known witch doctors in the area and I had to deal with some of them. The Islanders would go to the hospital for x-rays, and then take the film to the witch doctor for reading and treatment. I would say with certainty that the witch doctor could never read the film, and therefore not know what was wrong with the patient.

One patient I picked up was a very elderly island lady who was a practicing witch doctor. The hospital wanted her admitted for testing for cancer. I took one of our honorary officers (a T.I. boy) as a translator. This lady lived on the side of one of the high hills, it took about 200 hundred steps to reach her cottage. We finally got there and, oh boy, did we have trouble getting her out of the house. I tried all the tricks I knew and then some. Edward, the honorary, called me outside and ask me if I had seen the dirty rag she was holding, which I did see. He suggested that if I could get hold of that things would be well. I eventually did get hold of this very dirty rag and from that moment things did change. The lady was very compliant and we took her to hospital. I asked Edward what the significance of the rag was. It was apparently her good luck charm and she would never go anywhere without it.

SPREADING GOD'S WORD

While on the island we were involved in running a Christian mission programme, with the help of some Adventists who travelled from Cairns to assist. We ran 10 different programs over a two-week period. It was quite successful and I ended up with about 12 bible studies. Life just got busier for me, but God is good and I managed to continue with the studies for the time that we were on the Island. There is now a group meeting on Thursday Island.

Our time on Thursday Island was interesting and very diverse, but the family was not unhappy about being relocated back to the mainland. After 15 months on the island, I was appointed to the position of superintendent of Winton. We left T.I. at around the end of February and started at Winton. It was quite a change although I had already been out west previously.

WINTON

I commenced work at Winton in March 1980 and I went straight into organising the finances as the Centre was not very flush with cash. I had one officer working with me. His name was Doug but he was unfortunately not real fond of work. I set up a system for collecting subscriptions so that we could get a much stronger support base. Doug did not like the idea and said he was not prepared to visit all the properties. I advised him of my plan, I would do the collecting and he would have to handle all the ambulance cases that came in, with the assistance of my wife Heather, who was on the honorary staff. He was not happy with this arrangement, but, too bad Doug!

Winton covered a very large area and some jobs would take all day and even longer at times. We would occasionally take patients to Townsville which was about a seven-hour drive away. We also took many trips to Longreach which was almost two hours away.

I had a call once to a property several hours away west of Winton. The patient had a heart problem. In those days, we operated one man units. I would often take one of my children, especially to spot kangaroos. This trip, I had Alan with me, who was about 10 at the time. We got to the patient and he was primarily suffering from chest pain. I gave him some pain relief and made him comfortable in the back of the vehicle. I placed Alan beside the patient and told him to let me know if anything changed. We had travelled about an hour when Alan said the patient was "looking funny." I pulled up while we still had about an hour and a half before we got to the hospital. The patient was in fact having a cardiac arrest. What should I do? I was by myself with no medical assistance for hours if at all. I started CPR and fortunately revived the patient but we were still a long way from help. I decided that Alan would have to drive and I would look after the patient. Alan did a tremendous job of getting us to hospital, where the patient fully recovered. I put in a report with the case sheet detailing what happened, and was reprimanded by the head office. They told me I was never to do that again, but I told them that I will do exactly the same thing if it happens again. I also asked if they knew that the patient was alive and well. They replied telling me that I went outside the protocols. Okay, so what? I slept very well that night.

IF HE DIES SO DO I

I got a call to attend to a motor accident on the Opalton road, which was a very isolated area. The patient was an old opal miner known as "Wombat" because he lived with his missus, who was a full-blooded Aboriginal, in an opal cave underground. His injuries were not significant but he was knocked out for a long time. When we got to him, he was still out cold. I was loading him onto the stretcher when the missus turned up, seeing that Wombat was now lifeless, and thinking that he was dead, she started wailing and screaming.

She then picked up a big stick and donged herself on the head, rendering herself unconscious also. Now I have two unconscious patients to transport about 80 kilometres to the hospital. Better a full ambulance than a half-full one. Both of them survived their ordeal.

I DON'T SMOKE

My wife Heather was in the hospital one time when the Wombat's missus was admitted with a broken leg. She got to talking to Heather and soon after she worked out that Heather was married to the ambulance man. She wanted to thank Heather for what I had done for them. She had a tobacco tin which she wanted Heather to take. Heather replied that she doesn't smoke but it turned out that the tin was full of opals from their mine.

AN OASIS

I was once collecting over a very large area south of Winton. While collecting it was my habit to accept an invitation to camp at the station house, wherever I was, when it got towards evening. I called at an oil drilling rig late one day and was invited to stay the night, I was given a tour of the rig, and they also gave me lovely quarters for the night. They had a cafeteria, a restaurant, and a film theatre for staff. I had beautiful meals both for dinner and breakfast before I went back on the road.

Victor Torrens

ODD BEDFELLOWS

On one collecting trip, I called on a property fairly early one morning, just around 6am. I knocked on the door and was met by an elderly gentleman, the owner, who invited me in for breakfast. I was well fed and we did some talking during which I was informed that his wife of many years had passed away some time back. He then told me that he had a kangaroo as a bed mate, fair dinkum, it used to sleep on his bed every night. I suppose it would keep one warm. That's a new spin on the saying "hop into bed."

UPSIDE DOWN SEEDS

In Winton, it was very hard to do any good with gardening, as the soil was hard and so was the water. Anyhow, I had been told that all you needed was some Epsom salts in the soil and it would work. So I got some and also purchased some seeds at the local Newsagent, as that was where seeds were sold at that time. Planting then took place and the waiting started for the seeds to germinate. We waited and waited. Four weeks went by and we decided that the seeds were not going to grow. It must have been faulty seeds, so I went back to the Newsagent to complain. The owner stated that I was a lousy gardener and I apparently had put the seeds in the ground upside down. I did get a refund but never did any good with my gardening efforts in Winton.

PINCHED

Winton has a festival every two years. It was a major event that had a lot to do with swagman and "Waltzing

Matilda." The town council had a competition for the most inventive swagman. We entered one that was a paramedic, complete with stretcher and patient. We placed it on the roof of the station and lit it up with a spotlight. It also included an Australian flag. During the festival, we had about eight visitors staying with us, so we had people sleeping in every spare bed. At some point during the night, several University students from Townsville decided that they would "borrow" our stretcher and take it back to Townsville, as a souvenir of their time at the festival. These enterprising lads, all very drunk, scaled a 12-foot besser block wall, lowered the stretcher and mannequin down off the metal roof, within 10 feet of where my brother-in-law was sleeping, and pushed the stretcher up to the railway station, put it on the train and left town. I went out on a job a couple of hours later and saw that the stretcher was missing. I contacted the police who did some great detective work and found one of our local mechanics who had in fact seen the lads with the stretcher and actually drove around them in his car near the railway station. A phone call by the police to the railway station at Hughenden assisted in apprehending these lads with the stretcher in tow. I never pressed charges, but the lads did send the stretcher back with a $100 donation for the ambulance.

LOST AND OUT OF PETROL

I had family out for the Festival. My brother John, sister Sylvia, and her husband Ted. During this time, our boys owned a motorbike, which Alan had stripped and repaired. They had a lot of fun with this bike. They loved going bush and riding through rough country and creek crossings. I was never much good with the bike. There was one time when the boys were riding up a steep bank and I figured I could manage this as well. It was my turn and everyone was watching to see what would happen. Well, it did happen, big time. I took off with full power up the creek bank and completed a full roll over with the bike on top of me. Nothing was hurt except my pride. We decided to ride the bike out to Opalton while taking turns with a pillion rider. At this time, there was a car rally out and back to Opalton, involved with the Outback Festival. The Lions club was involved with carrying extra fuel for the cars and water for the hikers and other people. We were about halfway there when Ted and Nigel took their turn and away they went. They managed to take a wrong turn and found themselves on a lonely track heading west instead of southwest. While they were on this track they had an emu run alongside them for some distance. The road surface was mainly sandy and very slippery. After about 40 minutes, they decided that they must be on the wrong road, and just then the bike decided that it had gone far enough. Fortunately, there was a small reserve tank of fuel and they were able to head back to the way they came from. Fortunately for them, one of the Lions club vehicles also took the same wrong turn and they eventually met up. Fuel was taken on board and drinks were given, some drinks were hard, while others were soft. It took several hours before the intrepid bike riders were reunited with their worried family. This made a good campfire story.

COOKED

One cold winter night at about 3am, I got a call to a case at what I think was the Federal Hotel in the main street of Winton. Around the back of this pub there was a fire pit about eight feet across which they kept going through day and night, primarily to keep the patrons who wanted to sit outside on the log seats nice and warm. Most of the nights it worked well but during this night there weren't many patrons about. An Aboriginal was there with a couple of his mates and they had been drinking quite well, so this fellow went to sleep near the fire, which was lit by gidgee coals which as we know are always very hot. At some point, his mates left the scene to go home leaving this old mate by himself, curled up beside the fire. As we often do while sleeping, this chap rolled over and his knee was placed very close to the fire. It started cooking very slowly like a spit roast. We didn't know how long he had been in this position but we assumed that he could have been like that for a couple of hours. When I got there the knee looked like a roast pig, cooked well but not burnt. The patient was not in pain as the grog supplied plenty of anaesthetic. He was treated and taken to the hospital, then he was transferred to Brisbane for further treatment and he lost his leg to just above the knee.

SAVAGE DOG

Alan was given a blue heeler cattle dog while we were in Winton. It was a solid dog who apparently worked very well with cattle. The problem was it was as savage as anything. Even its owner could not go near his Ute without first making sure that the dog knew that it was him. The dog was no good as a pet and Alan was upset that he could not keep it. I arranged for him to go to a cattle property up in the Gulf country, where he settled in and apparently was very good with the Brahman cattle up there.

Victor Torrens

BUYING THE FARM

While at Winton in 1981, Heather and I decided to buy a small property as security if ever I suffer a bad accident. We were often at risk at work with the high-speed driving and with the contact with violent patients. We went to Brisbane and looked around at a few properties while on holiday but we had no luck. After the holidays, we headed back to Winton. We pulled up in Blackbutt to get some lunch and spotted some land at Mt. Binga for sale. We went and had a look and we were impressed, though we had to make a hasty decision. We asked if we could stay on the block overnight for a better look around the next day and it was all good. We liked the block, it was lovely country, with red sandy loam soil and a very good water supply from springs. We rang the bank and got approval to buy with the proviso that the bank will have to inspect it first. We made an offer and headed straight back to Winton. Our offer was accepted and so we became land owners. From then on every holiday was spent to work on the farm. We owned this place up until 2015 when we had to downsize due to Heather becoming unwell. A lot of lovely memories were made there. We had many family reunions and campfires, with people camping all over the place. I even made a nine-hole bush golf course, which provided much fun.

WRONG AMBULANCE AND SPEED BUMPS

I went to Crae-Crin station one afternoon to attend to a farm accident. When I worked at Hughenden, Crae-Crin was in their area, so when the people dialled Winton, they knew me and thought I was still at Hughenden. I responded as they needed an ambulance, and I took my brother-in-law with me for the drive. He was amazed at the hospitality shown by the station owners to us. It turns out that the Hughenden ambulance was also called and they got there first and took the patient to Hughenden, so there was no patient when we arrived, but there was time for a cuppa. This station was on the dirt road between Winton and Hughenden that had just been graded and was good for 100kph. At 5am the next morning, I left for Townsville which was a seven-hour drive away. I was with an elderly lady patient and we were sailing along in the one tonne ambulance when we were suddenly flying through the air. The old lady hit the roof of the car and said, "That was a big bump." Indeed, it was, because during the night someone placed an 18-inch high speedbump right across the road, illegally of course. However, on my return from Townsville, the road was back to normal.

COLD WATER SYSTEM

The town water supply for Winton comes from artesian bores and comes out of the ground. It is hot enough to boil corn meat or turn condensed milk into caramel in the tin after only a few minutes. Anyhow, this is where we got our water and it is too hot even for a shower. The solution is for homes to have a cold water system where several 44-gallon drums are placed in line under the house and bore water flows in one end and comes out reasonably cool at the other, just about right for a shower. The bore water is not great for drinking straight from the tap, but is quite good when cooled in the fridge.

SLIM DUSTY

I went for a walk around town one afternoon. I liked to walk whenever I could as it was difficult to have an exercise regime when one works 24 hours a day. Down one of the back streets I came across a fellow having a cuppa on the footpath, campfire and all to boil the billy. I got talking straightaway with Slim Dusty. He told me that he gets sick of drinking tea made out of an electric kettle, so he goes outside and lights a campfire in front of the motel. Slim was a nice chap.

SO CLOSE AND YET!

I went to Cloncurry with Heather for a QATB Conference one weekend. While we were on the way home on Sunday evening, we had 2 flat tyres, which left us no spares. At about 11pm when we were around 25 kilometres from home, we had another flat. We decided to contact the Centre and get young Doug the Ambo to bring out another spare for me. We did not have mobile phones in those days, so we resorted to using radio, both CB and UHF, but we could not reach Doug at all. We did get someone out near Broome West Australia who was monitoring the UHF emergency radio. He asked how he could help, and I asked him to ring Doug on the landline and reverse the charges. It almost did not work as Doug said he knew no one in Broome and he was about to hang up on the man. I eventually got my spare and we were able to get home safely. I could see the lights of Winton while all this was going on.

Winton was a great place to work as was any area I worked at as a paramedic. This was because I enjoyed my work and I was readily accepted into the community. My wife and family also provided great support at all times, wherever we were living and working. Heather supported me by learning first aid and becoming an honorary officer. It was good value for me and for her as well to get involved.

FIRST DOUG DUG A HOLE

Doug, the first officer who worked with me at Winton, was an older man, but as I have said he was not very energetic. The committee was forced to sack him after quite some discussion over holidays and long service. He had a very funny outlook regarding his entitlements and would not consider changing for anyone, so he had to walk. We then appointed another paramedic who was also named Doug. He was Canadian, and was a delight to work with. He walked with a distinct limp because of a previous accident. Doug drove an older Holden which he called the Golden Holden, because of its colour. One time we went out to Lorraine Station 15 or so kilometres out on the Longreach road as they had a carnival going on to raise funds for the ambulance. There was a raffle where the first prize was a roundtrip of Australia via Greyhound coach. Doug was lucky enough to win this, so he arranged for some holidays so that he and his wife and their two boys could take the trip. They went as far as Perth and decided they had enough bus travel so they purchased a new van over there and drove it home.

EGG ON MY FACE

Every year, the QATB would be audited by the Government Auditor who was nicknamed "barbed wire." Word would get around that "barbed wire" is on the way and all books had to be brought up to date. In 1982, I had a visit from the auditor and all was good, the books were in order and all funds were accounted for. A few weeks after he left I had to do a monthly reconciliation of the books, and for the life of me I could not get a proper balance. I blamed the auditor for doing something I could not find. After a lot of hours and a roll of calculator paper, I decided that I better get some help, so I contacted Jim Scrimgeour who was the financial officer of the council, and was also on the ambulance committee. He told me to bring the books down and that he will have a look at them when he gets a minute. I walked them down about two blocks away and gave them to him. I walked home and Heather had a message for me to contact Jim. The first thing he said was, 'how many months there are in a financial year'. Obviously there are 12, I told him. He told me that I have been trying to reconcile the books with 13 months in the year. What I was doing was very simple, I closed the books from when the auditor was due and started afresh when he left, therefore ending up with 13 balances for the year. I was a paramedic, not an accountant. But it all worked out right in the end, even the egg on my face.

SUTURE REMOVAL

My brother-in-law Ted Bakke came for a visit just after his gallbladder surgery. He rang from Brisbane to see if the hospital had a staple remover for sutures, and I confirmed that they did. He was here for a couple of days and we had to remove every second staple in a massive cut across his abdomen. We went to the hospital but were unable to find the staple remover so we decided to use some pointy nosed pliers for removal. Poor old Ted was not happy. He complained about the pain and the rough surgery, but we got the staples out and removed the others a few days later. He healed up alright. No problem.

CAMPED AT DAGWORTH STATION

I had the privilege of spending a night at Dagworth Station northwest of Winton. This was where Banjo Patterson wrote "Waltzing Matilda." The Elliots are lovely hosts and we had a good visit. I was doing the rounds collecting subscriptions and donations for the QATB at Winton. I did see some billabongs while there, but no swagman.

BOARDERS

It was at Winton where we had several of our wayward kids living with us, and at one stage we were approached by the publican of the Middleton hotel, asking if we could put his three boys up for a while and send them to school. Heather agreed so they moved in. They were nice boys who never gave us any trouble at all. We found out that after the eldest one left school, he became a member of a travelling group of Australian male strippers. We also bought a lovely old horse from their father. This horse was previously a very competent drafting horse who won many trophies. "Whiteman" lived with us for many years on the farm at Blackbutt.

STANTHORPE

In 1983, I thought it was time to try for a promotion and move to a larger station with more staff. I applied for several positions and was eventually appointed to Stanthorpe. We went from one of the hottest places to the coldest in Queensland. Little did we realise the change we would experience.

Victor Torrens

We packed up and arrived in Stanthorpe mid-October 1983. I settled in quite quickly, with four staff members and a good committee, reasonable equipment, and vehicles. It was great to have support officers available. When I read the previous minutes of the committee meetings it seemed that there was some discussion on the fact that I was a Seventh-day Adventist and they thought that I would not work on Sabbath. The chairman of the committee, Andy Jamieson, a retired army man, still said that they should give me a go. I am glad they did, although we wondered why I was appointed there, as it was the last on my list of places to work. God had His hand over the whole thing as there was need for some leadership at our church. Before the year ended I was appointed as Senior Elder, a position I held on and off for several years.

FUNDRAISING

There was quite a lot of raffle programs held at Stanthorpe to finance the running of the station. As I had started a collection system in Cloncurry, Hughenden, Thursday Island and Winton, which all worked as I had set one up initially in Caboolture which financed the station pretty well, I decided to have the same system at Stanthorpe and therefore cut out any raffles. One of the staff, a lovely guy named Cliff Vichie, offered to do the collecting for three months of each year, so we purchased the required stationary and also a station wagon, this way we did not have an ambulance vehicle tied up. It was a great success as I had expected and within 12 months, the staff did not have to run any raffles, although the ladies' auxiliary continued for a few years. The station became very financial over my time there. The staff members also increased from five to eight.

SETTLING IN

Work here was quite different from the other places I have worked at. We didn't have to travel such great distances to attend to any trauma or severe cases. The work load was greater though. I was always thankful that I had good staff who were willing to work and share the load, although I always did my share and then some, as a good leader should. The superintendent before me was not well spoken of by the staff. Sometimes though they did not know how to react to my leadership and the committee was also surprised with my way of running the station.

HANG THE BOSS

Not long after I started there, I came out one morning to the plant room, where hanging from the ceiling was a mannequin dressed like a superintendent. It was hanging from the rafters in the garage. I found it funny and we all had a good laugh, as the staff had finally become familiar with me and my work practices. Although a couple of them almost had kittens when I came there, they said that I would most likely sack the lot of them. The job was one which needed some humour, even if it was a bit dark.

A SNOW JOB

In July of 1984, we had some very heavy snow, and coming from Winton we really felt the cold. Heather and I had previously kitted us all out with tracksuits and parkas and the necessary cold weather clothing, but it was not enough for the snow, so we hit the shops again. It was a wonderful time with the snow, and our children had never even seen hail. Snow was an eye opener for them and for us both. We built a six-foot-high snowman in the backyard and went driving in the snow for a look around. The snowman stayed around for a few days.

EXPENSIVE ACCIDENT

During the snow, people were coming up from Brisbane to have a look and play in the snow. One chap who was not so lucky drove up from Brisbane in a brand new BMW which he borrowed from his showroom. He got as far as Brayside and while watching the snow, he lost control and fell over the side of a bridge. Nothing was hurt except for his pride and pocket. There were several accidents during this time with people not knowing how to drive in the snow, which is somewhat similar to driving in bulldust and sand.

Not long after arriving in Stanthorpe, the family decided to venture out to "the pyramids" for the day. We packed lunch and off we went. We decided to try and climb the pyramids, which are a group of giant basalt boulders hundreds of feet high. It was a strenuous task, yet the kids did it quite easily, but Dad, being a little older, struggled. At about the half way mark I was huffing and puffing, but a couple of reasonably plump late teenage girls were sitting on a small boulder and they encouraged me to keep going. I did not reach the top this time but I later did on a rescue we had to do.

Over my seventeen years here we were involved in several rescues in the pyramids' area. We generally had to do these rescues manually as vehicles were not suitable and the helicopter was not always available. One job involved a patient who had suffered a cardiac event right at the top, on a wet day. This made the rescue even more eventful as the rocks were very slippery. A lot of manpower was used that day, ambos, firies, police, SES, and others. We had the patient on a stretcher and ropes were used as support as we carried or slid the patient down the side. This type of rescue is generally carried out with helicopters now, but back then it was every man on deck. This type of work is also very hard on the shoulders of the people carrying in these conditions, hence the problems I am now having with shoulder re-constructions.

DID NOT CONNECT

I got called to a job out on Texas road about 40 kilometres out of town one afternoon. We were advised that there may be guns involved, which is always scary. When we arrived there, police were in attendance. We had to park about a kilometre away from the scene. The story was that a man and his two teenage sons were in the house and the father had threatened to shoot them. It was a waiting game. The father eventually let the boys go and they told us what had happened. Yes, there were guns involved but the father, while attempting to kick one of the lads in the bum, missed and slipped over and badly broke his leg which rendered him useless. We were able to treat the patient and it turned out to be a domestic brawl, which was a regular problem.

GUNPOINT

I received a call at about 1 AM to a domestic disturbance near Severnlea. I passed the police on the way out as they were returning from another job. I arrived at the gate which was closed, it was pitch dark and I was by myself. I opened the gate and as I was about to drive through and up to the house, suddenly there was a knock on the window of my car. I could not see anything until I wound the window down. I was suddenly staring into the barrel of a gun. A voice asked me, "Where are you going?" I responded, "Home." "That's good," said the voice. I put the car in reverse and headed home, just up the road I contacted the police who came back. It was a domestic and the lady of the house had been belted up, fortunately she was not shot. I reckon the Lord gave me the response needed that night. There were a lot of European farmers around Stanthorpe who would not hesitate to shoot if provoked. I know that because I picked a few of them up after their fights. The whole episode was a bit nerve wracking.

NOT ALWAYS SUCCESSFUL

All the staff were out on jobs around the district one morning and Heather was looking after the station. A car screeched to a stop in front of the plant room and a desperate woman raced in with a baby in her arms. The baby was found underwater and was unresponsive. Heather called one of the local doctors, and started CPR on the child who was about 3 years old. The doctor arrived but they could not revive the child. It was very traumatic for all who were concerned.

HOW FAST CAN HEATHER DRIVE

Another job Heather was involved in concerned a small child with asthma. Heather had been on the honorary staff for several stations we had worked at and she was competent. This job required her to transport the patient with an escort nurse to Toowoomba hospital for treatment. On the way, the patient deteriorated and needed urgent treatment that was not available in the ambulance, so the foot had to go down to get to the hospital rapidly. Heather was in the Toyota Hi-Ace and she apparently got it revved up enough to satisfy the nurse escort. They arrived at Toowoomba and the child was treated successfully.

HARD TO FORGET

While working at Stanthorpe, Heather and I went to the Sunshine Coast for a break. While there, we visited Aunty Mable and Roy in Nambour. We went to Petrie Park at Woombye for a toilet break. I went for a walk along the bank of Petrie Creek and somewhere there in the scrub was some clown older than me who I guess was a sex maniac. I was at this time a man of about 50, and this grub was walking along the bank in the opposite direction. When I got level with him he stuck out his hand and grabbed hold of my testicles. I said, "Keep going and I will break your arm." I probably would not have been able to as I was on the edge of an eight-foot drop into the creek and that is where I would have ended up. But he did keep walking. I was in shock and now I appreciate how easily someone can feel violated. This chap was in an old Ford car with his wife, so what he had in mind I do not know. I do remember that he was dirty and unkempt as was his wife and car when I saw them together shortly after the incident.

ACCIDENT PRONE

I was called to an accident involving a truck loaded to the hilt with all sorts of bits and pieces. It had rolled out the Summit way. This truck was travelling from NSW to Sunshine Coast with a lifetime of gear. Sitting on top of the load was an old forklift, and the load was scattered all over the place. The driver was treated for a broken arm and taken to hospital, and he was very lucky. Two days later, we were called to another accident, a car rollover at the same place. You won't believe it, but it was the driver of the truck, who had brought his family up to see where he rolled the truck. Nobody was injured this time. About three years later, I received a letter from an insurance company asking for a report on this chap and his accident. I had to write and ask them which accident they wanted a report on as he did not tell them about the second one.

OOOOps

It was 1:30am when I received a call to a car wrapped around a light pole. There was one young fella with a few injuries, none of which were life-threatening. The boys in blue asked the drunk man if he was driving and he told them no. They asked where the driver was but this young fella did not know. A search of the car revealed who owned it and an address. The police went around to the house and found the driver, who had no injuries, except for his pride. Upon further questioning, the police ascertained the reason he left the scene of the accident. It was because he had pooped his pants. He was charged with drunk driving.

WHICH WAY BOSS

I employed an older officer at Stanthorpe and he had no sense of direction. Here are a few of his indiscretions. I once sent him to attend the Triathlon at Storm King Dam on a Sunday. It started at 6am, so off goes the officer, looking forward to a day out at the dam. I received a call from the organisers at 7:15am, asking where the ambulance was. I did not know so I sent another man and vehicle and endeavoured to find out where Ambo 1 was. I tried calling on the radio and through mobile phones but I received no response. After some time, I got a call from Texas telling me that they heard our fellow on the radio and I asked him to call me. He did and promptly stated that he was at the intersection of Texas and Inglewood road west of Stanthorpe and he asked me whether he should turn left or right. I asked him to return to the station. You see, he had gone west from Stanthorpe instead of east, and was about 60 kilometres from where he should have been. Another incident occurred when he was the superintendent of St. George station and we had met at Roma for a regional ambulance conference. At the end of the conference at about 3:30pm on a Sunday afternoon, I had to drive our committee men back to Toowoomba where they were going to continue back to Stanthorpe and the super from St. George was to pick me up in Toowoomba and we were going to Brisbane for two weeks of training. I settled in to Toowoomba for what I thought might be an hour or so of waiting, as this chap was going to visit his sister in Chinchilla. So I waited and waited and waited, three hours went by and there was still no sign of my transport. Four and a half hours later, he turned up all flustered and concerned that I had to wait so long. What happened? He visited his sister in Chinchilla and when he left he joined the Warrego Highway and turned left instead of right and did not realise that he was going the wrong way until he was just 20 kilometres from Roma again. As a result, it was a very late night and not a good day in class the next day. His wife advised me that he was always going in the wrong direction almost every time they went driving.

BEWARE THE ANTS

I was called out to a motorbike accident early one morning just after daylight. The rider was thrown off his bike and ended up on a meat ants' nest. He had fairly severe injuries and was unable to move. He had been on the ants' nest for about 45 minutes before anyone found him on the dirt road and it took another 30 minutes before we got there. Boy, were those ants having a feast and there were still ants eating him when we got to the hospital. He survived okay.

GOLF HAZARDS

I played some casual games of golf at Stanthorpe with a couple of mates and my brother Ian who was stationed at Wallangarra with the army. It was an interesting golf course due to the amount of kangaroos and bearded dragons on the course. It was not uncommon to hit your ball and smack it into a kangaroo or see it bounce off a lizard and disappear into the bush. I also played at the Wallangarra Army Golf course several times.

BLACK/WHITE MAGIC

One weekday at around mid-morning, I got a call to attend a stabbing in Stanthorpe town. I was met outside the gate by a young lad who was about 10 years old. We asked him what had happened and he said he did not know, because his mother told him to go outside and play cricket. He complained that he could not play cricket by himself, but went outside at any rate. I went inside to have a look around while Frank went to get some gear. I found a Kiwi man with some stab wounds, none of them life-threatening. I started treatment but saw no sign of any other person. The patient would not say who stabbed him and he said that they would be caught and sorted out later. Frank was walking into the kitchen area when he suddenly stopped and pointed into the lounge room, and there in the corner was a white man we both knew with not a stitch of clothing on and painted from head to toe with white paste. It caused us a great deal of mirth. A large kiwi lady was eventually found and charged for the attack. We also found out that she was called the "Red Back spider," because apparently she would invite men home, spend the night in bed with them, and then attack them next morning. Lovely lady.

BIG BUSINESS AWARD

During my time at Stanthorpe, my staff nominated me for "Business man of the Year." I think it was in 1986, and my staff and I had worked hard and put the Centre into a very nice financial position and increased our staff numbers. I think the award was organised by the Queensland Government. Heather and I ventured into Brisbane for this great event. It was a black-tie event, and we were seated with some other hopefuls who were in big business. I did not feel too out of place, but I was also not in the race as the other companies were multi-million dollar businesses. The award was won by Leighton Holdings for their building programs. Still, it was amazing to be picked in the top 20 businesses for the state. We did have an enjoyable evening, all expenses paid.

Victor Torrens

IS IT EDIBLE?

I got called out one afternoon to an older couple who were not feeling well. We found them both in their beds, and there was vomit everywhere. It took us quite a while to find out the cause of their discomfort as they were very disoriented and confused. Eventually, we were able to work out the problem. They had some lovely "friends" who had come over for afternoon tea and brought a cake to share. The lady advised this couple that the cake was a savoury parsley cake, and they imbibed quite a bit of the cake before feeling unwell. We transported them both to the hospital with the remains of the cake. It turned out the cake was not parsley but marijuana.

FASHION CONSCIOUS

Lyn was a different lady, she was very nice, but different. She was a member of the Ambulance Committee for several years. When I say that she was different, I mean that she was different in her fashion sense. She was well-educated and was in a professional position, but she would do strange things with her hair. One day it would be red on one side, blonde on the other; another day it would be a chequerboard pattern or striped crossways in several colours. We never knew what she would have next. Her clothing was also generally different but the most bizarre thing she did was wearing odd socks and odd shoes to work often. She would wear one red shoe while the other was white or blue. This was her way of making a statement back in the 1990s.

THE END

In closing, may I say; the work of a paramedic is,- amazing – terrifying – thrilling – exhausting. It can hit the highest and the lowest points of emotion at almost the same time on the same case.

My career was very rewarding, mostly, but I had to concentrate on the good cases, which allowed me to retire as almost normal. When I say almost normal, I would like you to understand that the work of a paramedic is stressful, and many suffer from mind problems. I was grateful that my mind was not affected, so very much.

God was my strength and blessed many of my patients by giving me the knowledge and ability to treat them as best I could.

I trust that you, the reader, have enjoyed reading what I have written.

Thank you,
Victor M. Torrens (author)

www.ingramcontent.com/pod-product-compliance
Lightning Source LLC
Chambersburg PA
CBHW050318010526
44107CB00055B/2298